C000216575

Your Chinese Horoscope

Your Chinese Horoscope

JONATHAN DEE

Published by SILVERDALE BOOKS
An imprint of Bookmart Ltd
Registered number 2372865
Trading as Bookmart Ltd
Desford Road
Enderby
Leicester LE9 5AD

D&S Books
Cottage Meadow, Bocombe,
Parkham, Bideford
Devon, England
EX39 5PH

e-mail us at:-
enquiries.dspublishing@care4free.net

This edition printed 2002

ISBN 1-856056-32-5

Creative Director: *Sarah King*
Editor: *Clare Howarth-Maden*
Project editor: *Sarah Harris*
Designer: *Dave Jones*

Printed in Singapore

1 3 5 7 9 10 8 6 4 2

Contents

The Chinese Zodiac

The word 'zodiac' literally means 'circle of animals'. In the Western world, we use this word to describe the 'star' signs that divide our year into twelve equal segments. This stellar circle is not actually a circle of animals, however, because in addition to Aries (the Ram), Taurus (the Bull), Leo (the Lion) and others, we also include human figures, such as Gemini (the Twins) and Virgo (the Maiden), as well as a set of weighing scales, Libra. The ancient Chinese were more selective in their choice of symbols to represent their signs: their circle is a never-ending cycle of fauna only. Yet even they could not resist the inclusion of the mythical dragon in the system.

The familiar signs of the western zodiac.

The tradition of Chinese astrology is at least five thousand years old, and in its truest form it is very complex indeed. In the Western world, however, we have become familiar with the simplified version of the twelve animal signs, which was created in China in around the second century AD.

In accordance with the poetic nature of the Oriental world, there is a charming story that explains why individual years are under the auspices of particular animals.

The Twelve Animals of the Chinese Zodiac date to the 2nd century AD.

The origin of the animal signs

The Dragon is the only mythical beast in the Chinese circle of zodiac animals.

It seems that once, long ago, the Lord Buddha (although some say that it was the great sage Lao Tzu) decided to give a party for his favourite animals. In his wisdom, he knew that some of the animals were friends and that others were enemies, which meant that it would be difficult to get them all together in one place to resolve any difficulties between them. After much thought, the sage decided that he would name the years after the first twelve animals to arrive, in the order of their arrival.

When the animals heard the news they became very excited and set off at once, each determined to be the first and thus gain the highest honour. Initially, the tiger took the lead, his great speed ensuring that he outstripped his rivals. The tiger's pace soon began to flag as weariness overcame him, however, and the greater stamina of the ox ensured that he would be the victor. The ox duly reached the feet of the sage and bowed low in gratitude that he would lead the order of the signs. But fate plays a few tricks, and the ox did not know that the cunning rat had taken the opportunity to hide in the ox's tail. Before the ox's nose had touched the ground, the swift rat ran up the great beast's tail and along his broad back before jumping off the end of his nose, thus winning the race and becoming the first of the animals to bow before Buddha.

Buddha laughed so much at the antics of the rat that he immediately awarded the first year to him and the second to the resentful ox, with the tiger, hare, dragon, snake, horse, sheep, monkey, rooster, dog and pig following in that order.

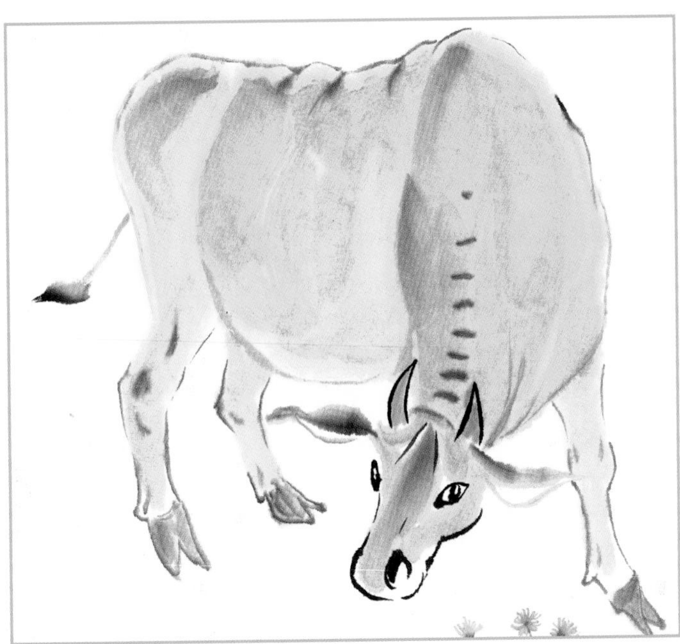

Variations in sign names

Some of the year signs are occasionally called by different names. The Rat may be referred to as the Mouse, for example, the Ox may be called the Buffalo or Bull, while the Hare is also called the Rabbit or (incorrectly) the Cat. In addition, the Sheep may be the Ram or Goat, the Monkey may be called the Ape and the Rooster the Chicken or Fowl, while the Pig may be described as the Boar.

How to work out your Chinese Horoscope

To work out your Chinese horoscope, first of all look up your year of birth in the table on pages 20 to 25, remembering that the Chinese New Year moves about between late January and late February. Note down the year's animal sign and element and also record whether the element is Yin (passive) or Yang (active).

To find out your animal moon, consult the table on page 9 and then look up the characteristics of that animal sign without reference to the element. Your character will be a blend of your year sign and your animal moon.

To find out the nature of your inner self, you need to find the animal of the double hours. Translate your birth time to Beijing time and then consult the table on page 10.

A man born in London on 1 September 1957 at 11.30pm was born under the year sign of the Rooster and his element is fire, which is passive, or Yin. His moon sign is also the Rooster (equivalent to Virgo), and his hour sign is the Hare (because he was born during British Summer Time, seven hours must be added to his time of birth to bring it in line with Beijing time).

A woman born in London on 17 August 1943 at 12.30am has the year sign of the Sheep and her element is water, which is passive, or Yin. Her birth-moon sign is the Monkey (equivalent to Leo), and her birth-hour sign (after adjustment to Beijing time) is the Dragon.

The hours and the moons

One of the questions that is commonly asked about Chinese astrology is, 'How can a sign covering a whole year of birthdays provide a full and accurate horoscope for anyone?' The answer is that there is more to it than that. The animal signs also govern the individual months, or 'moons', and the double hours within one day. Each of the animals is the equivalent of one of our more familiar, Western zodiac signs. All that you have to do is to translate your own star sign into its Chinese equivalent (see below) and then look up the characteristics of that sign in the relevant section.

The animal moons

WESTERN ZODIAC SIGN	CHINESE ANIMAL SIGN
Aries (the Ram) 21 March – 20 April	The Dragon
Taurus (the Bull) 21 April – 21 May	The Snake
Gemini (the Twins) 22 May – 22 June	The Horse
Cancer (the Crab) 23 June – 23 July	The Sheep
Leo (the Lion) 24 July – 23 Aug	The Monkey

Virgo (the Maiden) 24 Aug – 23 Sept	The Rooster
Libra (the Scales) 24 Sep – 23 Oct	The Dog
Scorpio (the Scorpion) 24 Oct – 22 Nov	The Pig
Sagittarius (the Archer) 23 Nov – 21 Dec	The Rat
Capricorn (the Goat) 22 Dec – 20 Jan	The Ox
Aquarius (the Water-bearer) 21 Jan – 19 Feb	The Tiger
Pisces (the Fish) 20 Feb – 20 March	The Hare

The animal hours

Just as the animal signs relate not only to a year, but also to a month, they can be applied to individual hours of the day, too. A purist would suggest that the only correct way of doing this is to translate one's time of birth into the equivalent time in Beijing. If you were born when Greenwich Mean Time was in operation, for example, eight hours need to be added to find the equivalent time in the Chinese capital. If you were born when British Summer Time was in operation on the other hand, seven hours should be added. For American births, add thirteen hours for New York and sixteen hours for Los Angeles. (If you are in any doubt, consult any Western astrologer, who should know about this calculation.)

Signs of the double hours

ANIMAL SIGN OF THE DOUBLE HOURS	HOURS (24-HOUR CLOCK)
Pig	23.00–1.00
Rat	1.00– 3.00
Ox	3.00–5.00
Tiger	5.00–7.00
Hare	7.00–9.00
Dragon	9.00–11.00
Snake	11.00–13.00
Horse	13.00–15.00
Sheep	15.00–17.00
Monkey	17.00–19.00
Rooster	19.00–21.00
Dog	21.00–23.00

The Five Elements

Apart from the animal signs, there is also a system of five elements in Oriental astrology, which differs somewhat from the four elements of fire, water, earth and air used in Western astrology. The five elements of the mystical East are wood, fire, earth, metal and water. These elements are also applied to individual years in groups of two years each (see the table on pages 20 to 25). The first year of each element group is considered to be the more active, and is described as Yang, while the second year is thought to be more passive, and is described as Yin.

WOOD	FIRE	EARTH	METAL	WATER

Yang and Yin

The concepts of Yang and Yin are basic to the Chinese belief system. Yang is an active, masculine, positive, light and energetic force. Yin, on the other hand, is the total opposite, being passive, feminine, negative, dark and heavy. This doesn't mean that you should think of Yang as being 'good' and Yin as being 'bad', however. Think of them like day and night, summer and winter or male and female. They are opposite and complementary, and neither could exist without the other.

Yang and Yin are usually symbolised by the well-known Tai Chi symbol, which extends the mutual opposition of Yang and Yin into a mutual dependence. The black dot in the middle of the white, Yang area is the seed of Yin, while the white dot in the black area is the seed of Yang.

Yang and Yin are equal and complementary opposites like day and night, summer and winter, active and passive.

When the concepts of Yang and Yin are applied to individual years, it can be seen that since two years of any element always appear grouped together, the first is considered to be Yang and the second Yin. The first year will be of a more active and outgoing nature, while the second will be passive and more contemplative. So now the five elements of wood, fire, earth, metal and water have been further divided into two distinct types. Every year therefore has a type (Yang or Yin), an element (wood, fire, earth, metal or water) and an animal sign (the Rat, Ox, Tiger, Hare, Dragon, Snake, Horse, Sheep, Monkey, Rooster, Dog or Pig), revolving in an endless cycle.

The element of wood

In ancient China, wood-type people were the intellectuals, and wood is the element of philosophers, teachers, students, lawyers and doctors. Education is very important to this type, and in modern times wood people usually gravitate towards careers in computing, electronics, science and communications. Many are very interested in philosophical subjects, religion and spirituality.

Wood gives you a powerful value system and high standards and ensures that you will be ethical and influential. You will be more compassionate and caring than your animal sign might indicate.

Wood type people are usually intellectual by nature, often involved with electronics.

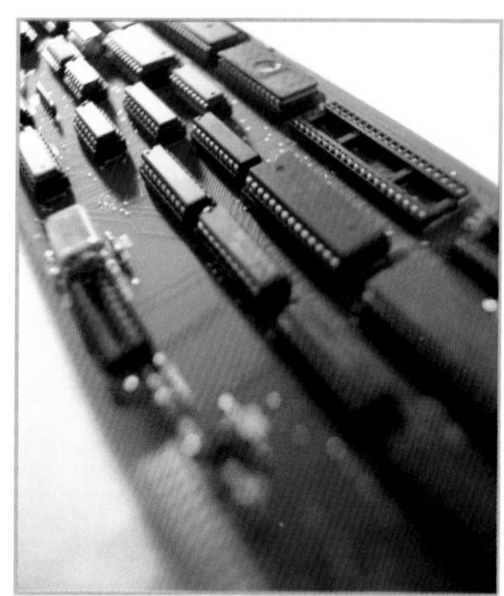

YANG WOOD – 'THE OAK'

Don't try to pull the wool over the eyes of an oak person! Astute and clever, they will quickly see through any subterfuge. They are responsible, hard-working and self-motivated people who rely on their own judgement. Oak people will thrive in any career that requires a quick and well-organised mind. Romantically, oak-type people are honest and straightforward; they hate mind-games and

Oak people are hard working and self-motivated.

will never forgive emotional blackmail. However, they do need to be left alone to do things in the way that they think is correct and cannot bear being dictated to.

YIN WOOD – 'THE WILLOW'

Like the willow, these people tend to bend with the wind. Willow people are capable of extreme empathy and can put other's needs before their own, frequently losing out in the long run because they didn't look after their own interests. They don't often ask for recognition and are real softies when it comes to romance, often being put upon or made to feel the victim in a relationship. In the spiritual stakes, however, willow people's karmic bank balance scores highly.

Those born in a 'Fire' year have an attraction to the uniformed services.

The element of fire

The element of fire was traditionally ascribed to the warrior class of ancient Chinese society, although these fiery types were also entertainers, acrobats, athletes and those who took part in public events, such as parades. Today we are as likely to see a fire person on the stage or television as we are to see one in the armed services, fire service or police force. People of this element often make a particular cause their own and publicly identify themselves with it, hence the association with uniforms, badges and insignia.

Fire will make your character stronger, endowing you with aggression and energy. It will make you more assertive, adventurous and passionate. You must beware of recklessness and impatience, however.

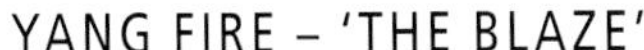

YANG FIRE – 'THE BLAZE'

People born in a 'Yang-Fire' or 'Blaze' year are often excellent cooks.

These are people who do not beat around the bush. They are open and forthright, impatient and hot-tempered – blaze types charge at everything. They are clever at picking up new knowledge in double-quick time and will be extremely impatient with anything that gets in their way. If courage and action are needed, someone born in a blaze year will provide it. Some say that blaze people are also excellent cooks.

YIN FIRE – 'THE FLAME'

The flame type of person is more of a showman than the blaze. Less interested in adventures, this type typically prefers a 'showbiz' lifestyle to military spit and polish. Always the centre of attention, this type dazzles by force of personality and witty repartee, but may also be a smooth-talking con artist. Flame people understand the public mood and will adapt to appeal to it.

'Flame' type people go to great lengths to be the centre of attraction.

The element of earth

Prudent Earth people excel at farming and cultivation.

In ancient China, those born under the element of earth were traditionally builders, farmers and keepers of water buffalo. In our age, this categorisation tends to be very similar, the earth person's fields (if you will pardon the pun) being construction, manufacturing, farming and food production generally. The element bestows stability, shrewdness in business, a long memory and also a generous nature.

Earth is a practical influence, making you patient, prudent and conventional. The earth element increases ambition and bestows efficiency and administrative abilities. The basic nature tends to be placid and slow to anger, but unforgiving of a hurt.

YANG EARTH – 'THE GRASSLAND'

These people are rather conventional, living comfortably within the structures of their particular society. They usually have physical strength, a great capacity for hard work and a talent for leadership that can lead them into a position of authority and honour. As may be imagined, 'grassland' types are sensual and 'earthy' in sexual affairs. They are not very romantic, however, preferring reliability to empty, but pleasing, gestures of affection. Careers in banking, insurance, finance and security will afford 'grassland' people splendid opportunities.

'Grassland' people are shrewd and very good at finance.

The creation cycle

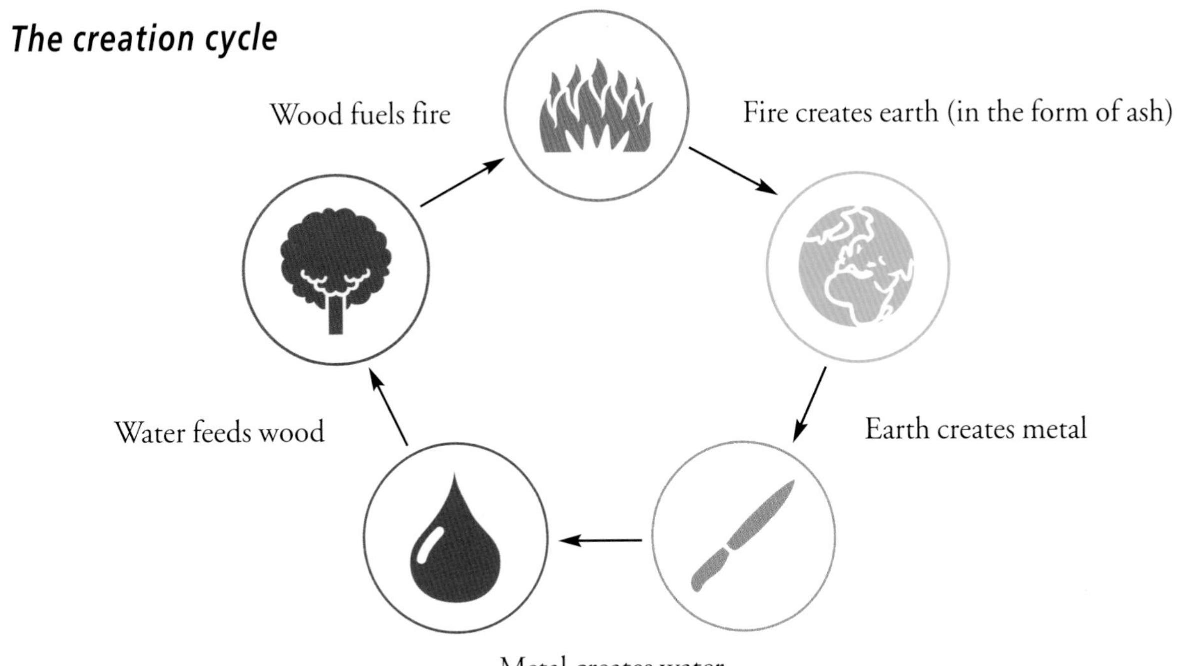

The destruction cycle

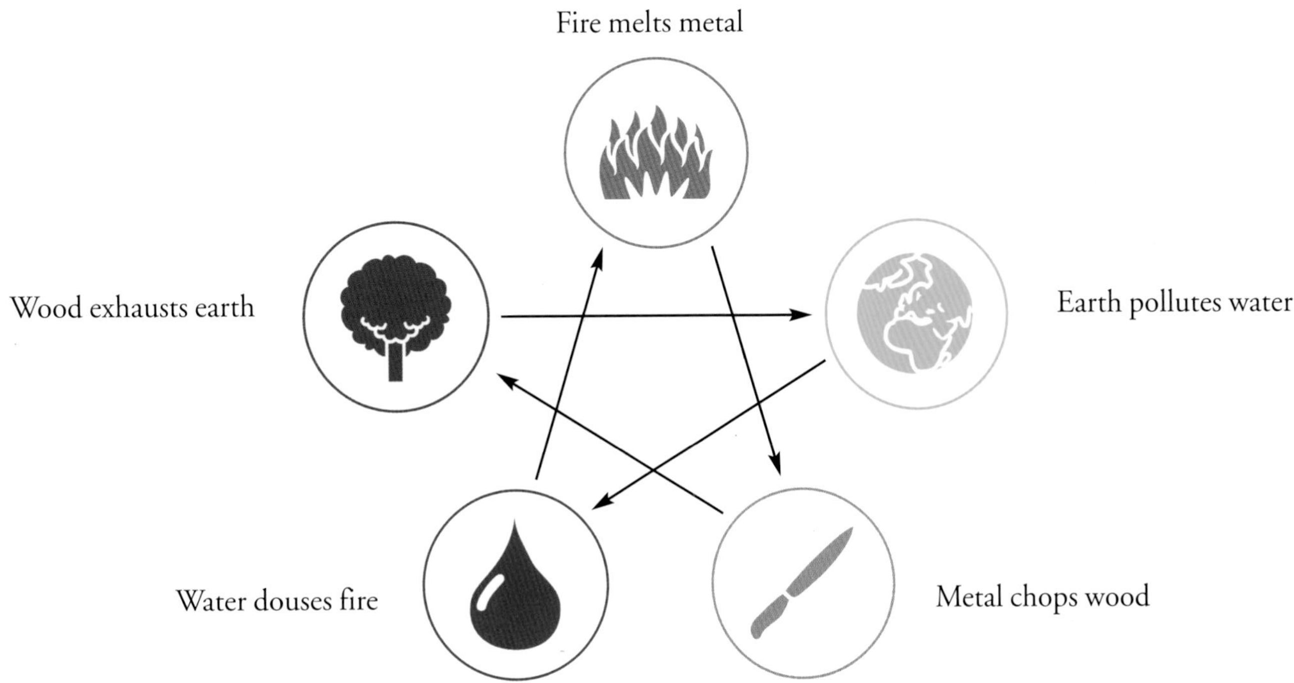

Your Oriental Birth Year

The Western calendar officially places the start of the Oriental year at 4 February, and this date can be used as a rough guideline when determining the Chinese New Year. However, the actual date of the Chinese New Year changes from year to year because it starts with the appearance of the new moon in either late January or February. Knowing the exact date of the Chinese New Year is of little importance unless you were born around this time, so take especial care if you are looking up an Aquarian birth date. It is, however, acceptable to regard an Aquarian as belonging to the sign that governed the previous Oriental year, even if he or she was born after the new moon that marks the transition. If in doubt, look up the information given for both year signs and make your own mind up about which sign you are influenced by.

To find your year type, element and animal sign, you simply need to locate your year of birth in the chart below.

YEAR	STARTS	YEAR TYPE	ELEMENT	ANIMAL SIGN
1930	29 JAN	YANG	METAL	HORSE
1931	17 FEB	YIN	METAL	SHEEP
1932	6 FEB	YANG	WATER	MONKEY
1933	25 JAN	YIN	WATER	ROOSTER
1934	14 FEB	YANG	WOOD	DOG
1935	3 FEB	YIN	WOOD	PIG

1936	24 JAN	YANG	FIRE	RAT
1937	11 FEB	YIN	FIRE	OX
1938	31 JAN	YANG	EARTH	TIGER
1939	19 FEB	YIN	EARTH	HARE
1940	8 FEB	YANG	METAL	DRAGON
1941	27 JAN	YIN	METAL	SNAKE
1942	15 FEB	YANG	WATER	HORSE
1943	4 FEB	YIN	WATER	SHEEP
1944	25 JAN	YANG	WOOD	MONKEY
1945	12 FEB	YIN	WOOD	ROOSTER
1946	2 FEB	YANG	FIRE	DOG
1947	22 JAN	YIN	FIRE	PIG
1948	10 FEB	YANG	EARTH	RAT
1949	29 JAN	YIN	EARTH	OX
1950	16 FEB	YANG	METAL	TIGER
1951	6 FEB	YIN	METAL	HARE
1952	26 JAN	YANG	WATER	DRAGON

1953	14 FEB	YIN	WATER	SNAKE
1954	3 FEB	YANG	WOOD	HORSE
1955	24 JAN	YIN	WOOD	SHEEP
1956	11 FEB	YANG	FIRE	MONKEY
1957	30 JAN	YIN	FIRE	ROOSTER
1958	18 FEB	YANG	EARTH	DOG
1959	7 FEB	YIN	EARTH	PIG
1960	28 JAN	YANG	METAL	RAT
1961	15 FEB	YIN	METAL	OX
1962	5 FEB	YANG	WATER	TIGER
1963	25 JAN	YIN	WATER	HARE
1964	13 FEB	YANG	WOOD	DRAGON
1965	1 FEB	YIN	WOOD	SNAKE
1966	21 JAN	YANG	FIRE	HORSE
1967	9 FEB	YIN	FIRE	SHEEP
1968	29 JAN	YANG	EARTH	MONKEY
1969	16 FEB	YIN	EARTH	ROOSTER

1970	6 FEB	YANG	METAL	DOG
1971	26 JAN	YIN	METAL	PIG
1972	15 FEB	YANG	WATER	RAT
1973	3 FEB	YIN	WATER	OX
1974	24 JAN	YANG	WOOD	TIGER
1975	11 FEB	YIN	WOOD	HARE
1976	31 JAN	YANG	FIRE	DRAGON
1977	18 FEB	YIN	FIRE	SNAKE
1978	7 FEB	YANG	EARTH	HORSE
1979	28 JAN	YIN	EARTH	SHEEP
1980	16 FEB	YANG	METAL	MONKEY
1981	5 FEB	YIN	METAL	ROOSTER
1982	25 JAN	YANG	WATER	DOG
1983	13 FEB	YIN	WATER	PIG
1984	2 FEB	YANG	WOOD	RAT
1985	20 FEB	YIN	WOOD	OX
1986	9 FEB	YANG	FIRE	TIGER

1987	29 JAN	YIN	FIRE	HARE
1988	17 FEB	YANG	EARTH	DRAGON
1989	6 FEB	YIN	EARTH	SNAKE
1990	26 JAN	YANG	METAL	HORSE
1991	14 FEB	YIN	METAL	SHEEP
1992	3 FEB	YANG	WATER	MONKEY
1993	22 JAN	YIN	WATER	ROOSTER
1994	10 FEB	YANG	WOOD	DOG
1995	31 JAN	YIN	WOOD	PIG
1996	19 FEB	YANG	FIRE	RAT
1997	7 FEB	YIN	FIRE	OX
1998	28 JAN	YANG	EARTH	TIGER
1999	16 JAN	YIN	EARTH	HARE
2000	5 FEB	YANG	METAL	DRAGON
2001	24 JAN	YIN	METAL	SNAKE
2002	12 FEB	YANG	WATER	HORSE
2003	1 FEB	YIN	WATER	SHEEP

2004	22 JAN	YANG	WOOD	MONKEY
2005	9 FEB	YIN	WOOD	ROOSTER
2006	29 JAN	YANG	FIRE	DOG
2007	18 FEB	YIN	FIRE	PIG
2008	7 FEB	YANG	EARTH	RAT
2009	26 JAN	YIN	EARTH	OX
2010	14 FEB	YANG	METAL	TIGER
2011	3 FEB	YIN	METAL	HARE
2012	23 JAN	YANG	WATER	DRAGON
2013	10 FEB	YIN	WATER	SNAKE
2014	30 JAN	YANG	WOOD	HORSE
2015	20 JAN	YIN	WOOD	SHEEP
2016	8 FEB	YANG	FIRE	MONKEY
2017	28 JAN	YIN	FIRE	ROOSTER
2018	15 FEB	YANG	EARTH	DOG
2019	4 FEB	YIN	EARTH	PIG
2020	24 JAN	YANG	METAL	RAT

The Rat

THE SIGN OF CHARM

1936, 1948, 1960, 1972, 1984, 1996, 2008, 2020

LOVERS

Love is likely to be found with those of the most compatible signs: the Ox, the Monkey and the Dragon.

FRIENDS

Tigers, Snakes, Dogs and Pigs will prove good companions, as will other Rat personalities, even though there will be a little friendly rivalry.

ENEMIES

Rats and Horses tend to loathe each other on first sight, but Roosters and Sheep are just tolerable to Rats.

WESTERN ZODIAC EQUIVALENT

Sagittarius (the Archer).

RULING PLANET

Jupiter (known as the 'year star' or the 'wood star' in Chinese astrology).

LUCKY GEM

Carbuncle.

SYMBOLISM

The Rat symbolises shrewdness, enterprise, wealth and abundant prosperity.

The characteristics of the Rat personality

The formidable Rat person is assertive, intelligent and impatient. Although they usually don't mean to upset others, it must be remembered that to a Rat only the Rat's desires, ambitions and needs are important. If this makes the Rat personality sound unpleasant, they do have some redeeming features, paramount among which is their sense of humour, which renders it almost impossible to be angry with them for long. Another positive side is the immense charm and gallantry that a Rat can display. One thing that is absolutely certain is that a Rat will succeed, even against appalling odds. They may not look like realistic contenders, but the extent of their achievements is staggering, an accomplishment which gives rise to amazement, admiration, respect and envy in equal measures. There is no doubt that Rat people have complex natures. On the one hand they are tasteful, refined, stylish and sociable. On the other, they are nervous and fear failure, a neurotic trait that every self-respecting Rat will attempt to conceal.

Rat people have a pronounced sense of humour.

The wood Rat (1984)

Insightful and ambitious, this type is well aware of where public taste is going and will usually get there before the masses catch up. Typically an excellent communicator, the wood Rat is caring, romantically inclined and artistically creative. On the minus side, this type of person has usually endured a difficult early life and is in need of emotional support.

The wood Rat is extremely creative and often shows artistic talent.

The fire Rat (1936, 1996)

The fiery nature of this Rat is never happier than when fighting tooth and nail for a cause. The fire Rat has a crusading spirit, strong ideals and a chivalrous character. This is fine in times of excitement, but when life is slow this Rat is often bored. Often witty, the fire Rat is a stranger to diplomacy, may lack self-discipline and can be moody.

The earth Rat (1948, 2008)

Financial stability is what matters to the earth Rat. Solid, thorough, hard-working and patient, this Rat will achieve success. Early marriages tend to be disastrous, however, and their relationships with their children may suffer. Even so, they will not be happy until they have established a family, usually later in life, when the financial pressure is off and they have made something of themselves.

Early marriages are often unsuccessful for earth Rats.

A metal Rat person often possesses an athletic physique.

The metal Rat (1960, 2020)

The metal elemental bias inclines the Rat to be very idealistic, wise and shrewd when making investments, although a metal Rat person may also be too money-minded or calculating in relationships. Metal sometimes engenders emotional turbulence and jealousy in the Rat person, also enhancing an athletic physique and making them a bit of a show-off.

The water Rat (1972)

The intellectual capabilities of the water Rat are awe-inspiring. No matter how impoverished their background, they will inspire respect and go far. These are very diplomatic sort of Rats, although they are quite

Water Rats love travel and are inspiring influences.

capable of cleverly getting their points of view across. They are also shrewd and quite critical, sometimes appearing unfeeling. Lovers of travel, water Rats need good companions in order to be happy.

The year of the Rat

Because it is the first sign of the Oriental zodiac, the year of the Rat is a time for new beginnings. Although the start of the year is notable for the sense of optimism and enthusiasm that it brings, it is not advisable to race ahead regardless: some groundwork has to be done long before any results can be seen. Remember that anything that is started in the year of the Rat will have long-term consequences, possibly lasting right through the full twelve-year cycle of animals. This means that the Rat year is also one for laying down the foundations of, or doing the preparatory work for, anything worthwhile that will stand the test of time. If there is something that you've always wanted to do, but the opportunity never seemed to present itself, this year will provide it. This is also true when it comes to nurturing hitherto neglected talents and for a general sense of renewed vitality.

The fortunes of the Rat

The world couldn't be a better place when the Rat is in its own year! Happiness, success in whatever you turn your hand to and a chance to express your amorous nature are all promised. Nothing can be thrown at you that you can't handle, but that doesn't mean that there are no dangers. Getting above yourself or becoming too self-satisfied would not be a good idea.

The **year of the Ox** is likely to herald a lot of hard work for the enterprising Rat. Fortunately, you are no stranger to that, but does it really have to be so relentless, so time-consuming and so demanding? The simple answer is 'yes' on all counts! The rule this year is to keep it simple. You may be confident, but don't overburden yourself with the

The year of the Ox is likely to be a hard struggle for the Rat.

unnecessary. This will be a good year if you are a clever and frugal Rat.

It's a time of competition, uncertainty and insecurity in the **year of the Tiger**, and the Rat will need all of her wits about her if she is to make a success of it. Things that seemed so static and unchangeable only a year ago will now fall victim to sudden upheavals, but at least the Rat is nimble enough to ride the waves of change. Whether you prosper or not will be up to you, and your cleverness, when the tiger roars.

In the year of the Dragon, the Rat's social life will be very exciting.

One of the alternative names for the sign of the Hare is that of the Cat, and cats generally don't like Rats (or mice), so be very cautious in the **year of the Hare**! In any battle of wits, the usually clever Rat is likely to be outwitted, which just goes to prove that there's always someone cleverer somewhere. The trouble is that this year is likely to throw you into the company of cunning and unscrupulous people.

At last the Rat will be appreciated during the compatible **year of the Dragon**. As long as you know your place and don't try to push yourself forward too much, you will prosper. Your social life in particular will be a crazy whirl of excitement. Even better than that, the contacts that you make will help you to further your ambitions. Add to this mix the heady delights of romance, and the Rat will have an ecstatic year!

The dramatic **year of the Snake** will probably be quite fraught for the Rat personality. Domestic issues are likely to be troublesome, and many Rats will feel that the only peace that they'll get will be outside the

A Rat mustn't waste money in the expensive year of the Horse.

confines of their homes. Unfortunately, their working life will be turbulent, too. All these problems can be lessened if you are truthful, honest and discreet, and if you do need a confidante, choose one with great care.

If you've been a clever Rat and have put something away for a rainy day, you will be happy during the **year of the Horse**. If you have been an extravagant Rat, however, and have spent the lot, you'll regret your folly because the Horse year will be expensive. It's also likely that doorways to loans, credit agreements and mortgages will be firmly shut in your face, so it will be down to you and your essential acumen to get yourself out of this mess.

The more creative the Rat person, the better during the artistic **year of the Sheep**. However, even if you aren't particularly creative you'll find all of the love, understanding and sympathy that you could possibly need in this most gentle and understanding of years. This is the year in which you should look to the future, forget past failures and put your best foot forward. Quash any feelings of pessimism and instead resolve to make your mark on the world.

Prepare for a whirlwind of excitement during the wild, madcap **year of the Monkey**. Rats will be amazed at how easily they achieve success this year, with everything seeming to fall into their laps, despite very little effort on their part. You'll be able to dump your emotional baggage and replace it with a plethora of joyful surprises. It's a time of uncomplicated fun, so enjoy it!

Success will find the Rat in the Monkey year.

The Rooster year can bring lasting love to the Rat.

The world will seem a complex place during the **year of the Rooster**. Practical problems will abound, especially in connection with your finances. This should make the average Rat very gloomy, but there is another side to the coin: in amorous affairs, the Rooster will point you in the direction of lasting love. Keep your eyes peeled, though, as the perfect partner might not be immediately obvious.

The Rat's finances should take a distinct turn for the better during the **year of the Dog**. And although some of your more exuberant, Rat-type habits will not win much approval, this will at least serve to focus your mind on the practicalities that will lead to eventual profit. Love isn't so well starred, however, and patience and mutual respect are needed if you are to make a success of a relationship.

The charming Rat can look forward to a time of plenty during the generous **year of the Pig**. Money will flow into your personal coffers and your innate financial acumen will ensure that a lot of it stays there. This doesn't meant that you won't enjoy your affluence – far from it: the Rat is a sensual beast and will indulge himself to the full during the course of this very profitable, fun-filled and easy year.

牛 The Ox

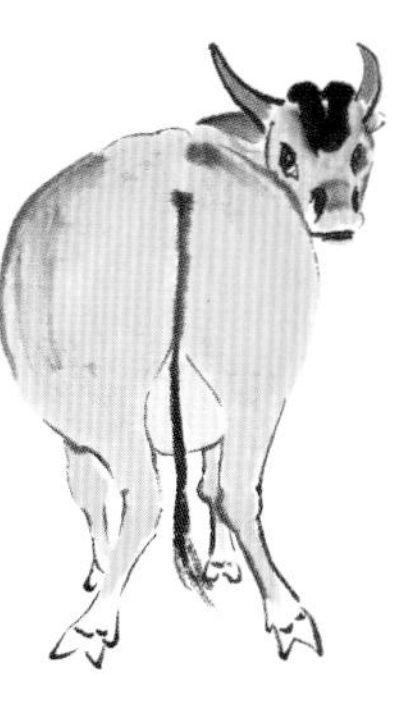

THE SIGN OF TENACITY

1937, 1949, 1961, 1973, 1985, 1997, 2009

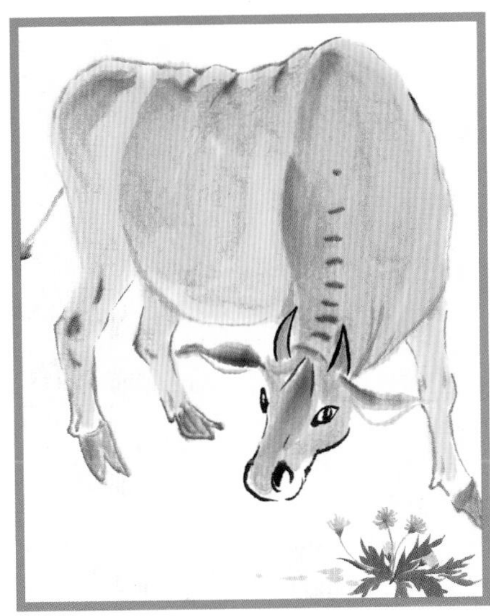

LOVERS
happiness can be found with those born in the years of the Snake, the Rooster and the Rat.

FRIENDS
other Ox people, Dragons, Hares, Monkeys and Pigs will be good friends.

ENEMIES
the unassuming Ox will feel threatened by the fierce Tiger and the exuberant Horse; the Ox hates the extravagance of the Sheep and the pessimism of the Dog.

WESTERN ZODIAC EQUIVALENT
Capricorn (the Goat).

RULING PLANET
Saturn (known in Chinese astrology as the 'earth star' or 'great regulator').

LUCKY GEM
white onyx.

SYMBOLISM
the Ox represents enduring prosperity through continuing effort.

The characteristics of the Ox personality

Ox people are home loving and devoted to family life.

Oxen are open-minded, practical people who take life in their stride and are seldom ruffled by the unexpected. The aura of calm, steady progress that they project can be something of an irritation to those who prefer the world to race ahead at a faster pace. For their part, Oxen like an orderly existence, free of stress and too much passion. Oxen are home-loving and are usually devoted to their families. They are also materialistic, adoring luxury, good food, music, art and comfortable furniture. Their intrinsic materialism is rarely vulgar: most Oxen have excellent taste and arrange their surroundings superbly. However, some Oxen may allow their materialistic side to overwhelm their entire lives and can become covetous and miserly. Because Oxen hate change, continuity, rather than passion, is the keynote in their relationships. On the plus side, this means that Oxen are faithful lovers who rarely stray. Even better, the sensual side of an Ox person ensures that although passion may be lacking, imagination will not be. Ox people are traditionally said to be physically robust and clever with their hands.

The wood Ox (1985)

This fortunate Ox will be respected for his or her integrity and ethical approach to life. The wood Ox is sociable, very considerate and open-minded. Often happiest when working alone or on something innovative, the wood Ox person may achieve wealth and celebrity. Many wood Oxen come from poor backgrounds, but use their origins as a spur to achievement. They often spoil their children.

The wood Ox may achieve a measure of fame and celebrity.

The fire Ox (1937, 1997)

There is a touch of glamour about the fire Ox because this type is often drawn to show business or the media. Like all Oxen, the fire type is hard-working and materialistic. Ambition is a driving force, and the fire Ox may be overly fond of power and, in extreme cases, may develop a feeling of superiority. The fire Ox person has a very strong libido.

The earth Ox (1949, 2009)

The sincerity of earth Oxen is their most notable feature. They are also hard-working, sensible, practical, truthful and intensely loyal. Earth Oxen can put up with a lot of difficulties, persevere through them all and eventually come out on top. They may have a slight tendency to depression that puts a strain on an early marriage, however. Traditionally, it is thought that an earth Ox person's second marriage will be more successful.

Metal Oxen are often deep, philosophical and gentle souls.

The metal Ox (1961)

This Ox is extremely strong-willed, tough and determined. His or her early life may have had more than its fair share of upheavals, as well as spectacular highs and lows. This results either in a character that is gentle and philosophical or is expressed as hardened cynicism, arrogance, possessiveness and a lack of affection.

The water Ox (1973)

The water Ox person is usually accustomed to material comforts, but also to emotional impoverishment. This is an extremely realistic person, however, who will make the best of things, even in the worst of circumstances. Patient, calm and unflappable, this is a team player who works well with others. The only downside to the character of the water Ox is a tendency to be overly suspicious when in love.

The year of the Ox

The year of the Ox is an excellent one for marriage.

This should be one of the most stable years in the Oriental sequence, in which the results of previous efforts and ideas should be seen. The Ox teaches us that we receive the rewards of life in direct proportion to the efforts that we have put into it, which means that those who have wasted previous opportunities will not be rejoicing when the year of the dutiful Ox comes around again. Traditionally, this year is said to be a good one for making contractual agreements, which implies that it is an excellent year in which to get married. However, the proviso of the Ox year goes something like this: if plans have been well thought-out and arrangements have been made previously (such as during the year of the Rat), all will be well, but if spur-of-the-moment decisions are made, the outlook is not so good. Slow and steady progression is favoured during this year, so whatever you do, don't expect fast results.

The fortunes of the Ox

When the Ox is in his own year he will feel carefree and ready for fun.

When the Ox is in its own year the pressures of life will ease and you'll feel carefree and happy. So carefree, in fact, that, unusually for you, you may be tempted to do something risky. Don't worry: the momentary urge will pass, and you'll again find yourself capable of making far-reaching, sensible decisions that will last well beyond the Ox year itself. Change that which needs to be changed now, before life becomes complicated once more and you lose your impetus.

The **year of the Tiger** is not the most comfortable of times for the Ox because it is filled with upheavals, which worries the steady Ox. It's simply a case of too much going on at once, which means

that you won't know which way to turn or what to do for the best. If you can manage to keep your head down, to shut out the noise and chaos and keep your life simple, you will find the going easier.

At least the Ox's work ethic is respected during the **year of the Hare**, even if the arty refinements of the nibbling rodent don't inspire you. It's best for the Ox to work alone during this year because partnerships will turn out to be disappointing at best, and annoying at worst, with someone else getting the credit that should be rightfully yours. You may be advised to upgrade your image and get about more.

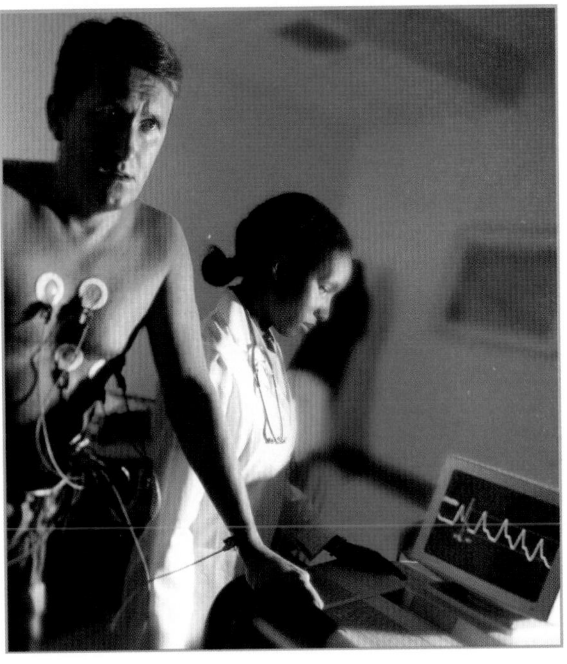

Too much good living may cause the Ox health problems in the Snake year.

The brash **year of the Dragon** is another uncomfortable time for the placid Ox, tending to wear on the nerves. There is bound to be a struggle for power this year, and it is doubtful whether the peaceable Ox personality is up to the battle. However, you can win in the tenacity stakes, so hang on in there because your opposition will tire eventually. This is a good year in which to make long-term plans.

The compatible **year of the Snake** should be a fairly pleasant one for the Ox, who will draw happiness from its calm, regular and controlled pace. Your finances should be particularly good this year, with the possibility that you will be able to save and even make a major profit. The only troublesome factor may be the general state of your health – perhaps all of the good living will go straight to the Ox's waistline.

The Ox will receive justified rewards for their efforts in the year of the Horse.

The **year of the Horse** is good news for the hard-working, persistent Ox because at last things seem to be falling into place. You will receive justified rewards for your efforts and may become more prominent in the world in general. However, you will have to be imaginative: the Horse has no time for the slow-witted, so get your thinking cap on and be creative.

One might think that the Ox would be happy during the **year of the Sheep**, but unfortunately this will probably not be the case. Your planning ability will go, only to be replaced

A hint of flamboyance is to be expected in the Rooster year.

by a vague feeling of indecisiveness that will exasperate any self-respecting Ox personality. The Sheep year has a quality of reeling from one minor crisis to another, which means that the Ox will have plenty to deal with, but little to show for it.

An immense capacity for flexibility is required in order to cope with the **year of the Monkey**, but the Ox does not adapt easily or quickly to the new. Although your fortunes should be generally good this year, you will only gain by staying abreast of current affairs, fashion and fads. However, you may be surprised and overwhelmed by a passionate love affair that is coming your way!

The compatible **year of the Rooster** dawns with the promise of ordered progress and sound planning. The Ox will feel at home during this year, and some of the Rooster's flamboyance may even rub off on you, helping you to slough off part of your staid image. Although you will be understood and appreciated for your skills and diligence, don't be tempted to toy with another's affections in case you receive an unpleasant surprise.

Take the opportunity to see the world in the year of the Dog.

The Ox will find a worthy ally in the Pig year.

For the Ox person, the **year of the Dog** is an excellent one in which to travel, see the world and increase your appreciation of the diversity of life. In business, too, it will pay to go further afield, to seek out new territories for expansion and conquest. The Ox can go a long way this year, both literally and metaphorically, so make the most of your new-found freedom. This is the year in which you know best, so ignore all criticisms.

During the **year of the Pig** it's likely that the Ox will find an ally, who may be self-seeking, but will also further your cause. It's a matter of linking up with someone whose aims coincide with your own, on either a personal or a business level, and perhaps both. Things speed up during the Pig year, and for once you will be happily picking up your pace. Those who know you may be astonished by your transformation, but had better get used to the new you!

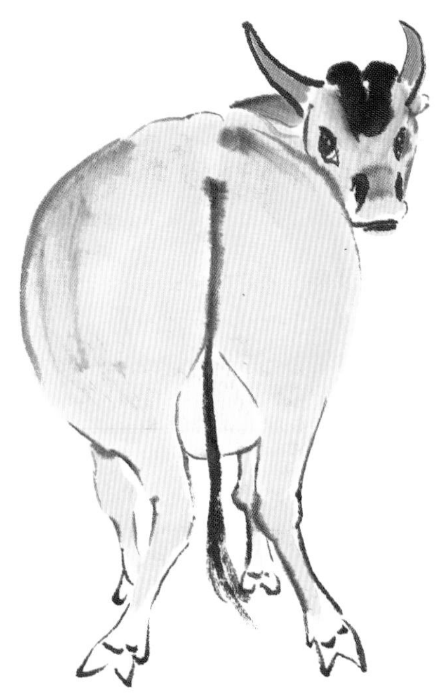

THE SIGN OF COURAGE

1938, 1950, 1962, 1974, 1986, 1998, 2010

LOVERS

fulfilling relationships may be formed with those born in the years of the Dragon, Horse and Dog.

FRIENDS

the popular Tiger makes friends with Rats, Hares, Roosters, Pigs and other Tigers.

ENEMIES

the cautious Ox, the guileful Snake and the chattering Monkey are not fond of the Tiger.

WESTERN ZODIAC EQUIVALENT

Aquarius (the Water-carrier).

RULING PLANET

traditionally Saturn (the 'earth star'), but now considered to be Uranus.

LUCKY GEM

sapphire.

SYMBOLISM

the Tiger represents optimism, humanitarianism and valour.

The characteristics of the Tiger personality

The pleasure-loving Tiger is humorous and cheerful.

The scintillating personality of the Tiger ensures that he or she is a fascinating person to know. Sociable to a fault, the Tiger is kind, humorous and cheerful, but don't be fooled into thinking that he or she is a pushover or a fool: the often flippant façade of the Tiger conceals enormous strength and ambition. This is not a character that is content with second best – the Tiger aims straight for the top! Tiger people are often self-employed or run their own businesses. Quite apart from a love of wealth and status, there is also a strongly rebellious streak in this jungle cat, who won't be able to abide toeing the line for someone else for very long. The Tiger has an amazing capacity for hard work, but an equally astonishing capacity for having fun, and those with less energy will soon be left behind in the Tiger's headlong (and hedonistic) rush through life. Tigers have expensive tastes, so it's just as well that their earning ability is so great. On a less positive note, Tigers may burn themselves out and become prone to stress-related ailments if they don't take time out now and again. Another of their less attractive features is their desire to be the centre of attention at all times.

The independent Tiger will often prefer to be alone.

The wood Tiger (1974)

Wood Tigers are easy to find: they're usually in charge! They love prominence and celebrity, but are frequently so independent that they prefer to live alone. Often artistically talented, original and inventive, wood Tigers will earn a respectable income. Family life may cause them problems, though, and estrangement from their parents is common.

The fire Tiger (1986)

There's no doubt that the fire Tiger is very clever indeed – perhaps a little too clever – always hatching devious plots and displaying a vast range of general knowledge. Like most Tigers, this type likes to be in the limelight, surrounded by the famous. Female fire Tigers are passionate and loyal, but also possessive and prone to jealousy.

The earth Tiger (1938, 1998)

Earth Tigers need to work hard from an early age to make something of their lives. These types usually leave home young and are well on the way to establishing themselves by their twenties. The earth Tiger person has the reputation of being a good leader, with sound judgement, who provides an inspirational example. In love, this Tiger is very faithful, but also possessive.

The earth Tiger is a hard-worker from an early age. They often leave home while young.

The metal Tiger (1950, 2010)

Metal Tigers are very lucky with money, but are rarely satisfied with anything that good fortune brings them, some going on to be very successful, but others frittering away their gains. Witty, eloquent and passionate, the metal Tiger is rather egotistical and prone to taking risks. Although they may be forceful and dominate their surroundings, they may lack a basic understanding of human nature.

The water Tiger (1962)

Born business people, water Tigers are shrewd, ambitious and persuasive. They have a good sense of humour and are generally regarded as being sincere and honest. Water Tigers are not good at tying up loose ends, however, and old problems may therefore come back to haunt them. These types are usually not good in relationship situations because they always find the grass greener somewhere else.

Metal Tigers dominate their surroundings and can be confrontational.

The year of the Tiger

The Tiger's rage will take the world by storm in a wild, turbulent year.

The rage of the Tiger will swiftly burst upon the world as this Oriental year begins. The Tiger is thought to be a turbulent sign, so it's no surprise that the events of the year will be wild and worrying, but all that one can do is to sit tight and hope for the best. Because the Tiger favours the intuitive side of life, logic and reason seem to take a back seat during this year. Follow your intuition, and perhaps you can get through it without too much flack flying in your direction. The impulsive will probably do well during this year because they are in tune with the Tiger nature. Traditionally speaking, those who do best during the Tiger year don't seem to be working to any plan whatsoever: they take each day as it comes, keep an open mind and are ready to react to any potential crisis at a moment's notice.

The fortunes of the Tiger

A whole decade opens up to the Tiger in its own year. Chinese tradition states that this is the year in which the Tiger can choose his destiny, so do so wisely. Because this choice is so important, fate will smile upon you and will give you an easy ride, along with plenty of leisure time in which to make up your mind. Your love life is the main arena for your good fortune, and because the Tiger is especially alluring and charming during its own year, don't waste your opportunity.

The **year of the Hare** is propitious for the Tiger personality. If you have made the right decisions in your own year, you will now start to see positive results. Although there may be the odd obstacles to contend with, you'll overcome them. In business affairs, you are bound to prosper and are likely to receive more recognition for your achievements. Don't boast, however: the best fortune is reserved for the discreet.

Although the **year of the Dragon** is likely to be a good one for the Tiger, remember that the Dragon is an absolute monarch who doesn't favour those who rock the boat. If you are to do well during this year (and most Tigers do), keep your more controversial opinions to yourself. Whatever

Tigers should travel widely in the Snake year.

you do, don't try to steal the Dragon's thunder. Stay businesslike and focus on your purpose without making a fuss.

The Tiger is likely to become irritated during the **year of the Snake**. Its sinuous pattern of events won't suit your direct nature, but slowing down a little won't do you any harm either. It's time to take life more easily, whether you like the idea or not. Travel more, see the world and take everything as it comes. Although monetary good fortune may not be evident, a romantic fling should make up for that.

The Tiger is under a compatible sign during the **year of the Horse**. Great triumphs await the daring Tiger, but any success will come at a price because too much glory all at once could encourage him or her to become insufferably self-satisfied and not above gloating over the misfortunes of rivals. It's best to work hard and not to allow overconfidence to tempt you into taking unnecessary risks.

The poor Tiger may find the events of the **year of the Sheep** completely baffling. The main problem is that the trend of public opinion will be totally contrary to your own, making you feel misunderstood and possibly somewhat picked upon. Your only realistic strategy is to retreat to wait for a time when your views are in fashion once again. Revolutionaries are at a loss when no one is prepared to listen.

Tigers will feel misunderstood and somewhat picked on in the Sheep year.

Tigers should find that the world is with them once more during the unpredictable **year of the Monkey**. You should now be able to achieve your dreams. No matter how crazy they may seem, you know that they are viable and, what's more, everyone will seem to agree with you. Be as independent as you like: take the lead, and all else will follow. Tell yourself that you are a visionary and can achieve great things.

The Tiger's social life will be a triumph during the dazzling **year of the Rooster**. You may not achieve much in a practical sense, but your tigerish feelings of self-worth will be considerably boosted by the expressions of admiration that you receive. Emotionally, the Rooster year is very hopeful, both for long-term relationships and for those that are brand new. Tradition states that any problems in your life will be short-lived during this year.

The Rooster year provides a boost to the Tiger's social life.

The Tiger will find that the Dog year is excellent for emotional commitment.

The **year of the Dog** should be a particularly good one for the Tiger. You will find that the world has moved into step with your own revolutionary views and will feel at home in this atmosphere of reforming zeal. You may find a like-minded partner during this year, and long-lasting love is in the air. In work affairs, although the going may be tough, you know that anything worth having is worth putting effort into.

The easy-going nature of the **year of the Pig** may fool Tigers into thinking that they can allow practicalities to slide a little. If so, this is a mistake: although some other signs will find their financial fortunes growing, Tigers will see theirs ebbing away. Refrain from making generous gestures and keep your eye on the accounts. Those Tigers who don't care about cash are likely to travel widely.

The **year of the Rat** is one in which Tigers should tighten their belts, live within their means and not – repeat not – indulge in overly idealistic scheming. The Rat does not approve of the Tiger's profligate ways and is too practical to be sympathetic to revolutionary fervour. All in all, be sensible during this year, invest safely and curb your tendency to be a spendthrift. It may seem boring, but just this once think of your future.

There are likely to be plenty of arguments during the stolid **year of the Ox**. Tigers don't mind that, however, and will be quite prepared to stand up for any point of principle, although they will mind losing! The Tiger's reforming zeal hasn't got much of a chance to shine during the year of the conservative Ox, so save your breath and keep quiet.

The Tiger will suffer financially unless he is very careful in the Rat year.

The Hare

THE SIGN OF VIRTUE

1939, 1951, 1963, 1975, 1987, 1999, 2011

LOVERS
love will be found with the artistic Sheep, the sensitive Pig and the loyal Dog.

FRIENDS
the Horse, Snake, Ox and Tiger are good friends of the Hare, but for real mutual appreciation, try another Hare!

ENEMIES
the ostentation of the Dragon and the outspokenness of the Rooster horrify the Hare, as does the excessive charm of the Rat.

WESTERN ZODIAC EQUIVALENT
Pisces (the Fish).

RULING PLANET
traditionally Jupiter (the 'wood star'), but now considered to be Neptune.

LUCKY GEM
chrysolite.

SYMBOLISM
the Hare represents longevity, virtue and prudence.

The characteristics of the Hare personality

The refinement and good taste of the Hare personality are beyond question. In fact, Hares have a reputation for aloofness and snobbery, but this is not always the case. Although it is true that Hares often stand back from others, this does not mean that they are snobs, only that they have an extremely sensitive nature and are easily upset by dramas. That having been said, to the world at large Hares appear self-assured, emotionally detached and seem to think of themselves as being superior. In many ways they are, being blessed with great intelligence and interesting looks and exuding an aura of mystery that many find alluring. In addition, the Hare is often psychic. There are usually two ways in which others react to Hares: they are either respected and admired or respected and loathed. The Hare's façade may be impressive, but serves to conceal a deep sense of inadequacy. A threatened Hare will react to hostility either by raging wildly or, perhaps even worse, by cutting their opponent to the quick with their cold sarcasm.

The wood Hare (1975)

At first glance there is nothing exceptional about wood Hares. They are not rebels, but conventional people who enjoy working as part of a team, as well as being compassionate by nature and rather intelligent. Some wood Hares may win renown as athletes or writers. Usually good with children, their compassionate character leads them unobtrusively to help out people who are less fortunate than themselves.

Wood Hares make good writers.

The fire Hare (1987)

The fire Hare person is likely to be rather emotional, intuitive, possibly psychic and a bit unconventional. Often found in the medical profession, some fire Hares take a more unconventional route into healing by practising alternative therapies. In general, they are popular, fun-loving and devoted to their families. They need security above all in relationships, and the same can be said for the way in which they handle their finances.

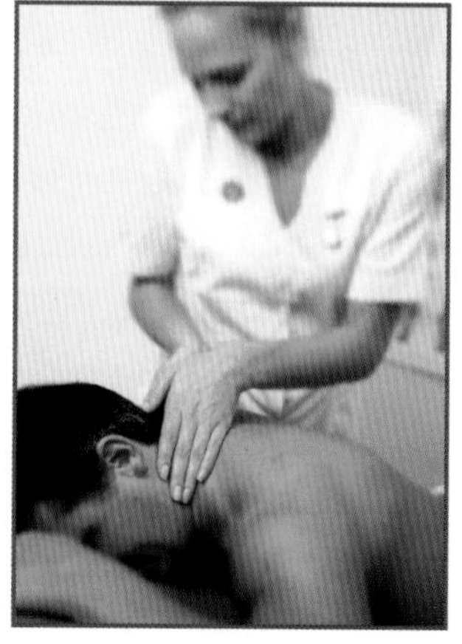

Fire Hares are often interested in alternative therapies.

The earth Hare (1939, 1999)

Easy-going earth Hares make an impeccable virtue out of ordinariness. These Hare types are logical and hold rationality to be the most important measure of life. They are not especially ambitious and are at their best when in a relationship with someone tougher and more determined than them. Cautious in their financial dealings, Earth Hares are devoted to family values and sound education.

The metal Hare (1951, 2011)

The metal Hare is a connoisseur, a collector or, if one is to be critical, a hoarder! Sometimes considered to be moody, these Hare types actually need privacy. This does not mean that they shun society, however – far from it: metal Hares generally make influential friends and allies. Metal Hares can be possessive in love and are generally very protective of those in their circle.

Metal Hares are collectors, probably hoarders who can't bear to throw anything away!

The water Hare (1963)

Sensitive water Hares are so emotional that they are easily upset. Often considered to be artistic dreamers, these types are romantic and very caring. An insecure lifestyle doesn't seem to bother them much, and many may be thought of as being bohemian. Water Hares are great travellers and can be relied upon to come up with imaginative tales of their adventures. Not noted for their ambition, they are usually content with what they have.

The year of the Hare

After the tumultuous Tiger year, the gentle, refined time of the Hare will come as a relief to many. Peace should reign, and this period may mark a time of reflection and harmony. This quiet year could frustrate those who wish to rush ahead, of course, but it is equally likely that this time of tranquillity, with progress being made without pressure, will be a blessing to others. In fact, those who put the interests of others before their own are likely to do very well during the Hare year, even if this is not

their primary intention. The year of the Hare is traditionally thought of as being good for all family affairs, especially for marriage and for increasing the size of your clan. It is also an advantageous time for the property market, with excellent investments and profits being made. The worlds of the arts, fashion and media are also emphasised during the Hare year, with innovative styles and methods coming to the fore.

The year of the Hare is a good one for buying property.

The fortunes of the Hare

Fate provides a wonderful opportunity for the Hare in its own year: a respite from past dramas and the chance to plan future moves in an atmosphere of calmness. Although the lure of social life will be strong, Hares would be foolish if they devoted all of their energies to enjoying themselves. In finances, keep a close eye on your out-goings and be warned that the possibility of someone trying to defraud you is not out of the question. On the other hand, it's good year for Hares who gamble. In love, communication is the key to happiness.

Hares who gamble will do well in their own year.

There's not likely to be much peace, calm or refinement during the **year of the Dragon**. The general atmosphere is one of brash flamboyance, and although Hares can play along with it, they won't always like it. In fact, it may be wise to

stand back from the folly that you'll see around you – it's a wise Hare who knows when to stay low and hidden. Hares are good at being philosophical, and this year will give them plenty of chances to prove it.

It's going to be a time for improving the mind during the **year of the Snake**. Intellectual pursuits beckon, and clever Hares will be able to further their education in many ways. It's also a year in which selfishness will be no bad thing, so stand aloof and ignore any criticism. Friends and family members may get themselves into trouble, but they'll also be able to extricate themselves from it without any interference from you. In addition, a more spiritual and meditative mood will appeal to you now.

The Hare will feel more vigorous and energetic during the busy **year of the Horse**, when your mind should be incisive and quick on the uptake. This is a particularly good trait to possess during the Horse year, which will see sufficient upsets happening to people around you to keep you alert. However, just because friends and family are in turmoil, try not to take on their problems – you'll have enough on your own plate!

Hares should indulge their more cultural tastes in the Sheep year.

Although your finances could be better during the **year of the Sheep**, you'll have very little else to complain about. The year of the compatible Sheep will enable Hares to express the finer side of their natures and to enjoy the pleasures of culture, music and art. You may find yourself moving among a different circle, one in which you will meet many kindred spirits.

Intellectual pursuits are the favoured activities in the Monkey year.

The **year of the Monkey** could be a worrying time for gentle Hares, but although it may be disruptive, the Hare's old defence of standing aloof will come in useful. The Monkey doesn't worry overly much about security, which means that Hares may feel vulnerable as changes suddenly occur around them. If you

want some peace, stay away from the centre of things, live quietly and engage in intellectual pursuits.

The financial stakes will be very rocky indeed during the hateful **year of the Rooster**. The Hare and the Rooster cannot be described as friends, so it could be a case of the Hare having to run and hide again. Because the Rooster has a way of pulling the rug from under you, especially where money is concerned, protect your assets well. This is another year in which you should bide your time.

A wise Hare will look after his money in the year of the Rooster.

The past few years will have rattled the sensitive Hare, so the **year of the Dog** should come as a relief. Things will calm down, life will become understandable once more and Hares should be on their way to prosperity, happiness and fulfilment. The trouble is that Hares are likely to be so shell-shocked that they won't realise it immediately and will still be looking around for trouble. Put your fears aside and start building up your confidence.

Happy Hares can buy, buy, buy in the profitable year of the Pig.

Luck is certainly with the Hare during the profitable and pleasurable **year of the Pig**. The Hare's innate taste and refinement will find perfect expression as the money comes rolling in, and you can indulge yourself by improving your lifestyle. Treat yourself this year and do whatever you fancy: buy some luxuries or go on an extravagant holiday – it's likely that love will find you on your travels.

The wise Hare should remain on guard

throughout the **year of the Rat**. It is said that paranoia is nothing more than a heightened sense of reality, and if that is the case Hares had better start practising a suspicious sideways glance because few people can be trusted during this year. Don't take chances or listen to plausible rogues: supposed inside information will be nothing more than a ruse to relieve you of your cash. Be careful!

Hard work and dutiful attitudes loom as the **year of the Ox** dawns. Glamour and refinement must take a back seat as Hares put their shoulders to the wheel. There's a lot to be done, but you should get through it all and come out the other side both better off and having gained a great deal of experience. Patience and effort are needed now, so take life at your own pace and make no major decisions.

It's time to ring the changes during the **year of the Tiger**. This sign is friendly to the Hare, so you will benefit from these progressions and revolutions. You may not be altogether comfortable with the upheavals, but you will prosper as long as you shift your stance and are ready to change your opinions. Adaptation is the key to success, and there is no doubt that the wily Hare will cope.

龍

The Dragon

THE SIGN OF LUCK

1940, 1952, 1964, 1976, 1988, 2000, 2012

LOVERS
those most compatible with the dazzling Dragon were born under the signs of the Monkey and the Rat. However, both the Rooster and the Snake will find the Dragon's charisma irresistible.

FRIENDS
the Dragon person will be happy in the company of the Tiger, Pig and Sheep.

ENEMIES
neither the Dog nor the Ox is in sympathy with the exuberant Dragon. Ancient tradition also claims that 'The Dragon flies to the clouds at the sight of the Hare'. Two Dragons together tend to fight, so it's unlikely that you'll live easily with those of your own sign.

WESTERN ZODIAC EQUIVALENT
Aries (the Ram).

RULING PLANET
Mars, which is known as the 'fire star' or the 'bright star' in Chinese astrology.

LUCKY GEM
amethyst.

SYMBOLISM
The powerful Dragon symbolises the inexorable course of destiny and the forces of nature. It was also used as the emblem of the Chinese emperor himself and, in a more general sense, as that of China.

The characteristics of the Dragon personality

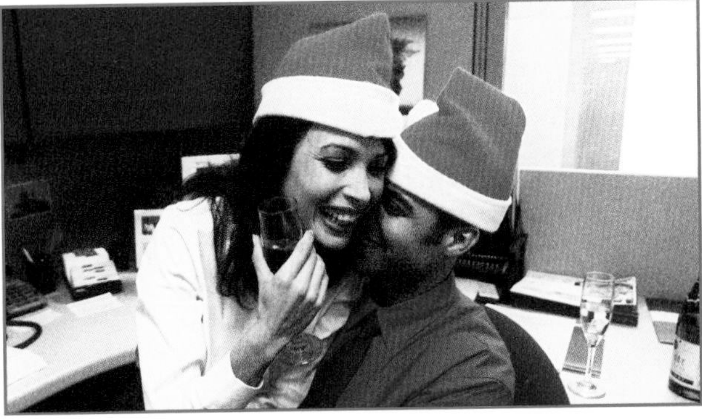

Dragons have an unusual, not to say unique, moral code!

People born in the year of the Dragon are proud, stylish, resilient, versatile and energetic, and the dazzling Dragon personality can easily impress or overwhelm shyer, quieter types. Dragons claim to possess high principles and are extremely honourable in their own way. However, the principles that they espouse can be very individual indeed, while their moral code may be only moral in their own opinion – which to them, of course, is the only one that counts! Dragon people often display a promiscuous streak and are capable of maintaining multiple relationships. Ambition is a great driving force, and Dragons will not allow anyone to thwart their plans. High-flying Dragons will often take risks to achieve their ends and have little patience with more cautious types. A display of panache and courage is all well and good, but if Dragons want to maximise their chances of success, they must develop their attention to detail.

The wood Dragon (1964)

The lucky Dragon often lives to a ripe old age.

The wood Dragon has a logical mind and can be extremely inventive and creative, but is often quite eccentric. Although they need to be admired, wood Dragon people often choose an independent lifestyle and may prefer to live alone. They like to be comfortable and live well and should enjoy a happy old age. Tradition states that wood Dragons of both sexes are ardent lovers.

The fire Dragon (1976)

This the most competitive, and occasionally argumentative, sort of Dragon personality. Fire Dragons are determined to get what they want, when they want it! However, their brash approach can be attractive and, like all Dragons, the fire type is charming. Adventurous, sociable and great fun to be around, fire Dragons can also be thoughtless and prone to accidents through lack of planning.

The earth Dragon (1988)

Those Dragons of the earth element simply know that there is only one correct way: theirs! Often tyrannical, earth Dragons are usually infuriatingly right. However, they are truly outstanding characters and are destined to move among influential people. Earth Dragons should never marry for money or status, otherwise family rifts will occur. If they marry for love, luck will come their way.

The metal Dragon (1940, 2000)

Metal Dragons are charming characters, even though they tend to be blunt and forthright in their opinions. Lovers of material wealth and the high life, metal Dragons are often obsessed by status and can also be prone to jealousy. Tradition maintains that female metal Dragons tend to be mean, while males are a little more generous.

Metal Dragons are lovers of material wealth and the high life.

The water Dragon (1952, 2012)

The water Dragon personality is extremely intelligent and honourable. Faithfulness in all dealings is paramount to this type. The Dragon arrogance is still present, however, and water Dragons take little notice of other people's views. They love to read, and females of this type are often drawn to psychic or spiritual matters. Water Dragons desperately need a soul mate to appreciate them.

The Dragon year

The scintillating year of the Dragon should be notable for events as extraordinary as the majestic beast itself. It should start with an amazing event, which will give a taste of what is to come. Tradition states that the end of the Dragon year will bring a repeat of the events that began it. In essence, any period ruled by this regal serpent is favourable to anyone who is willing to take a calculated

The Dragon year is going to be extraordinary, scintillating and exciting.

The Dragon symbolises the inexorable force of destiny.

risk. It is a time for discovery and adventure, sometimes dangerous, but also bringing the real possibility of high rewards. The grandiose nature of the Dragon encourages all of us to think big! It should also be borne in mind that the Dragon does not favour the lazy, those who avoid their responsibilities or who expect something for nothing. Symbolically, the Dragon represents the inexorable force of destiny, which means that many people will feel that fate has taken a hand in their affairs during this year. If the year of the Dragon happens to have an earth influence, it should be turbulent, with earthquakes and other titanic disasters being prevalent. (Fortunately we don't have to worry about that until 2048!)

The fortunes of the Dragon

When the year of the Dragon comes around, Dragon people can look forward to a period when success will find them. There is a sense that everything that you attempt will turn out to be a triumph – not necessarily in the way that you intended, but perhaps even better than you had planned for. Your dazzling personality should shine this year and you should be extremely attractive to others. Added to this is the promise of prosperity.

The Dragon can expect a power struggle in the year of the Snake.

The **year of the Snake** should see a continuation of the Dragon's good luck because the Snake and Dragon are symbolically related. However, there may be some petty politics and power struggles in store, both in your career and within your family. The Dragons who will do best will lie low, as well as developing a more philosophical attitude to life.

The **year of the Horse** is generally a lucky one for Dragons. Fate will take a hand in your affairs and for much of the time it will seem like a roller-coaster ride. The only real danger lies in the possibility that you will become so carried away by your good fortune that you will become arrogant and express your superiority in an inappropriate manner. This is a year for adventure and enriching your experience of life.

The Dragon will express boundless creativity in the Sheep year.

The **year of the Sheep** is one of inspiration and a chance to express the Dragon's boundless creativity. Those Dragons who are involved in the media will do very well, but even other Dragons will discover previously unsuspected talents. Only those who are willing to applaud the Dragon's every effort will be acceptable companions. Some so-called friends should be ditched now because they have a negative influence on you.

Unpredictability is the keynote of the **year of the Monkey**, when usually self-possessed Dragons may become rather insecure. A big risk is in the offing, and for many Dragons this will be a make-or-break time. Be patient: rushing ahead regardless invites disaster. Don't be too proud to admit to a mistake or to change a course of action that you instinctively know to be wrong. On a more positive note, the Monkey will add excitement to your love life.

Emotional turbulence is a feature of the **year of the Rooster**, and your commitment to a long-term partnership may be thrown into question. The Dragon may feel somewhat emotionally empty at this time, so concentrate on practical affairs, such as your personal security, investments and financial dealings in general. This is a good year for money matters, with long-term benefits accruing to the shrewd Dragon.

A wild and exciting love life is in store in the Monkey year.

It's important to put others first during the **year of the Dog** and to forget selfish concerns for a while. You may become involved in a crusade of some kind and many will have cause to be grateful for your efforts. However, this year is not conducive

to a happy love life, and cynicism within love affairs could cast a shadow over your mood. Emotions aside, you will eventually reap the benefits of your labours in more practical matters.

The outlook is excellent for the **year of the Pig**, when Dragons should find the appreciation – even adulation – that they've been seeking. Every sphere of the Dragon's life will see triumphant successes, and the luck seems never-ending. However, it wouldn't do to become too big for your boots or to alienate others simply because you are doing so well. When you're at the top of the tree, a little humility will win you a lot of goodwill.

The fortunes of the Dragon will receive a welcome boost during the **year of the Rat**, and the home is an area in which luck and happiness go hand in hand. If this were not enough, your love life should bring joy, contentment and security. Even the enormous Dragon ego can't fail to be satisfied by all of the flattery that comes your way. This year, the only danger area is your tendency to overspend outrageously.

Tradition is the keynote for the **year of the Ox**, but this does not suit the innovative Dragon, whose usual sparkle will be muted. A reckless Dragon would be well advised to stay as calm as possible and to think carefully before doing anything in order to avoid calamity. Some humble pie may have to be eaten, too, as the Dragon grudgingly takes a subservient position for a change.

Home life is a source of happiness to the Dragon in the Rat year.

Flattery might tempt the Dragon to overspend outrageously in the year of the Rat.

Dragons should be back to their usual, exuberant selves as the **year of the Tiger** begins. The Tiger enhances your zest for life and you'll be determined to live yours to the full, so enjoy yourself! This year is good for your financial fortunes, love life and adventures. You may also be rewarded for an achievement or act of bravery. Don't be too cocky, however, or you'll have cause to regret your boastfulness.

The **year of the Hare** is likely to be a quiet one for Dragons, which is hardly surprising following the excitement of the Tiger year. Dragons will no longer be in the limelight, and any attempt to push themselves forward will be met with resentment. Take your cue from the Hare and polish your manners, perfect a talent and make steady, unassuming progress. You may be rather bored, but your own year is coming up fast, so regard this year as a period of respite before the fireworks start again.

The Tiger year is excellent for the Dragon's financial fortunes.

The Snake

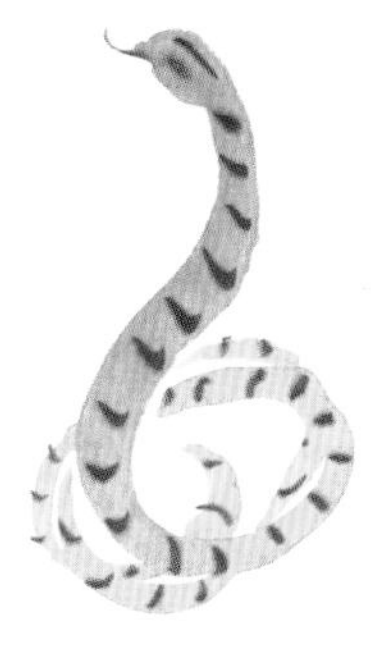

THE SIGN OF WISDOM

1941, 1953, 1965, 1977, 1989, 2001, 2013

LOVERS

the sensual Snake will find emotional happiness with the candid Rooster and the diligent Ox.

FRIENDS

Snakes are appreciated by those of their own sign, as well as Rats, Hares, Dragons, Sheep and Dogs.

ENEMIES

the sentimental Pig will irritate the Snake. In addition, according to Chinese almanacs, 'If the Snake catches sight of the Tiger, it is like being wounded with a knife'.

WESTERN ZODIAC EQUIVALENT

Taurus (the Bull).

RULING PLANET

Venus (in Chinese lore, Venus is called the 'metal star' or the 'great white').

LUCKY GEM

opal.

SYMBOLISM

the Snake represents, wisdom, glamour and cunning.

The characteristics of the Snake personality

The secretive Snake personality is very profound indeed and should not be underestimated. Beneath the attractive, graceful and stylish exterior is an exceptionally clever mind, capable of great concentration and, on occasion, extraordinary cunning. Not particularly sociable (unless, of course, being charming gets them where they want to be), Snake people hate useless small talk. They would far rather study and refine their knowledge than hang around with the stupid and the small-minded. Their secretive nature extends to both their personal lives and their financial affairs. On the subject of finances, Snakes are considered to be lucky, often coming into money through inheritances, divorce settlements, winnings or unexpected strokes of luck. In addition, Snakes are independent personalities who don't feel the need for approval and regard taking other people's views into account as being beneath them. A Snake's greatest dread is becoming totally dependent on someone else, while appearing foolish or weak would be almost as shameful.

Snakes often benefit from inheritances, settlements, winnings and strokes of luck.

The wood Snake (1965)

A difficult start in life is typical for the wood Snake person, with a youthful illness or poverty having made them security conscious. Wood Snakes are frequently fascinated by history, especially the intrigues and dark doings of yore. Often accomplished wits, wood Snakes hate chaos and crowded venues. They are also vain, especially about the state of their hair. Romantically, these Snakes are attractive, intriguing and very fickle.

The wood Snake hates the chaos of crowded venues.

The fire Snake (1977)

The domineering fire Snake is a force to contend with! Self-possessed, arrogant and opinionated, these Snakes have a larger-than-life personality that is impossible to ignore. They ensure that they move among influential people and their ambitions are boundless – but destined to be fulfilled – even though later in life they may regret the choices that they made. Their romantic natures are secretive and very self-centred.

The earth Snake (1989)

Fortunate earth Snakes gain luck through hard work. Conservative in their opinions, these serpents never lose sight of their goals. Order and precision are their watchwords, and they ensure lasting prosperity through their skill in business and property dealings. Because they may appear to be unfeeling, or even callous, earth Snakes need an understanding spouse.

Earth Snakes ensure lasting prosperity through shrewd business dealings.

The metal Snake (1941, 2001)

There's no denying that metal Snake people are difficult to get along with. Skilled and talented they may be, but they are also proud and secretive and may alienate those who would like to help them. They make good friends if you can get past their metallic exterior, but don't cross them because they are formidable and underhanded enemies. In addition, they are renowned for changing careers frequently. In matters of love, males tend to go for younger women, while females are attracted to older, powerful men.

The water Snake (1953, 2013)

Slithering through the corridors of power is the destiny of the fastidious water Snake. These Snake types are astute, intelligent and practical, with a creative or lateral view of life. Like other Snakes, they are ambitious, lucky and very charming. The water Snake is not very emotional, preferring the world of the mind, and therefore needs a partner who is similarly inclined.

The year of the Snake

Remarkable scientific breakthroughs are to be expected in the inventive year of the Snake.

Because the Snake is a fairly philosophical and introspective sign, in contrast to the brash Dragon the serpent will bring to light many questions of a deep and searching nature. The answers to some of these questions will not be easy or welcome, but the influence of the Snake means that these matters will nevertheless be pursued until all of the mysteries are fully exposed. The political world especially will feel the force of this process, with shocking scandals coming to light. Patience is the key to success in this year, and those who are content to allow matters to develop at their own pace will do well. The same cannot be said for the rash, those who wish to force issues and set their own, more speedy pace, who will have cause to regret their impetuosity. Traditionally, the Snake is said to be inventive, so there are likely to be remarkable scientific breakthroughs during this year. The serpentine good taste and sense of elegance will be evident in the way that fashion, music and the media set new trends.

The fortunes of the Snake

There is a danger of upsetting emotional dramas in the year of the Sheep.

The Snake its own year had better have its wits about it because opportunities will occur thick and fast and it wouldn't do to let any of them slip by. Although you may have big plans, you will have to get down to the nitty-gritty in order to make them work. Having said that, nothing is beyond you, and fortune favours you. The Snake year is also good for patching up old family disputes and restoring the peace.

The Snake is not very comfortable during the **year of the Horse**, when its usual strategies of subtlety and guile will not go down well. If you can manage to avoid complications, such as dealing with legal issues, so much the better, because success is unlikely in such instances. It is all too easy for others to misunderstand the Snake this year, so you will have to be open in your dealings and explain yourself clearly.

Upsetting emotional dramas are a recurring feature of the **year of the Sheep**. This unpleasant trend is made worse by the interference of unscrupulous people, who will take advantage of the Snake's goodwill – if you let them. There is a danger of being conned, not just out of money, but also in terms of other people taking advantage of your sympathy. Take care!

The **year of the Monkey** is a time when the Snake will need to be extremely diplomatic. You may find this active time confusing and won't always know which side of an issue to take, so it's important to remain cool and somewhat aloof from the neurotic goings-on around you. Your excellent taste may be compromised, too, circumstances forcing you to lower your very high standards for a while.

The **year of the Rooster** is eminently compatible with the nature of the Snake, and this will be mainly expressed in a renewed sense of financial well-being. Your subtle plans will find unexpected allies, who will help your cause. Your home life will be happy and your romantic nature will find ample opportunity for love. Although you may experience some ups and downs, your fortunes will be generally on the up.

The Snake will have a happy home life in the compatible sign of the Rooster.

In practical and financial affairs, the **year of the Dog** is a very promising one for the Snake. You may turn your hand to something new and exciting and may well be surprised by how successful this enterprise turns out to be. You'll also feel more attractive than usual, and your renewed self-confidence will enhance your style and elegance. If you can spend some time away from the hustle and bustle of the city, so much the better for your nerves.

Snakes will feel that they're on top of things during the **year of the Pig**. Feeling contented and secure, many Snakes will seek to upgrade their abodes, perhaps by moving to a better, more exclusive, area. Indeed, you may find that the more greenery there is around you, the better your quality of life. Any major decision must be well thought through, however. The Pig year may also see some insensitivity in your love life.

Snakes should get away from it all for a while in the Dog year.

In the year of the Pig, the Snake will find that the more rural the surroundings, the better his fortunes.

Emotionally, the **year of the Rat** could be quite challenging for the peace-loving Snake because its fast and furious events won't allow you much rest. On the other hand, these demands on your time and effort may prove to be financially rewarding. However, you'll wonder whether your loss of confidence, inner rage and lack of personal vision are worth the trouble, especially when your cash flow is nibbled away at the end of the Rat year.

The **year of the Ox** is unlikely to be easy for the Snake, although you will feel more in control and will be happier with its slower, less demanding pace. Money problems will be a recurring feature of the year, however, which can only be combated with hard work and dedication. Snakes may wonder why the universe seems to be picking on them, but I'd advise you to forget such deep questions and knuckle down to the job in hand.

They say that it's a funny old life, and the **year of the Tiger** will prove it! Snakes won't much like the unruly disorder of the raging Tiger year and must guard against small, silly accidents, especially during the early months. A little loss of serpentine dignity may be experienced as the mad scramble gets under way and the pace hots up, but the Snake has little choice but to charge along with everyone else.

The Snake will be in tune with the refinement that the **year of the Hare** brings. The lure of the good life will be strong, while the financial resources will be there to make it possible for you to better your lifestyle. This is also an excellent time for the Snake to express its adventurous side, travelling in style being a distinct possibility. Luxury and glamour are the keynotes of this year, so do everything with panache!

A wise Snake will take extra care of his personal and home security mid-way through the Dragon year.

During the **year of the Dragon** Snake personalities will find their world being bombarded with crises and dramas, but at least these will mainly happen to other people, leaving you to seek safety in your bolt hole. You may, however, experience your fair share of melodramas in your love life, although these will be unimportant. Take extra care of your personal and home security at midsummer.

馬 The Horse

THE SIGN OF ARDOUR

1930, 1942, 1954, 1966, 1978, 1990, 2002, 2014

LOVERS

a happy union can be made with the faithful Dog, the talented Sheep or the courageous Tiger.

FRIENDS

the Horse enjoys the company of Dragons, Snakes, Monkeys, Roosters and Pigs.

ENEMIES

the opportunistic Rat is too devious for the Horse, while the Hare is too snobbish. According to Chinese almanacs, 'The White Horse cannot share a stall with the Black Ox' – in other words, a Horse of the metal element cannot be happy with a water Ox.

WESTERN ZODIAC EQUIVALENT

Gemini (the Twins).

RULING PLANET

Mercury, known in Chinese astrology as the 'water star', the 'little regulator' or the 'delicate and brisk'.

LUCKY GEM

beryl.

SYMBOLISM

a distinguished career.

The characteristics of the Horse personality

Horse personalities are cheerful, independent, outgoing, often outspoken and possess immense charm. Most have a great sense of responsibility and will work very hard on behalf of their families and dependants. Another characteristic is their astonishing stamina, which leaves less hardy folk trailing behind, a trait that wins the respect of all who know them. Horses also have the reputation of being dextrous and, indeed, good at everything they do. Being so active, the Horse personality is a restless one, and many born under this sign are keen travellers. On a less positive note, Horses can also be impatient, capable of exploding over minor matters, sarcastic and prone to long, moody sulks if they don't get their own way. For these reasons impulsive Horses can damage their own best interests by alienating those who could help them the most. On the other hand, there is always the chance that the Horse can save the day by laying on the charm with a trowel.

The indefatigable Horse is a restless and energetic traveller.

Horse people are very responsible and work hard to provide a good life style for their loved ones.

The wood Horse (1954, 2014)

Fun-loving and extremely sociable, the wood Horse enjoys company and the great outdoors, preferring the country to the city and often working on the land. Those who settle down with a family are considerate, caring and protective, while the other wood Horse type enjoys freedom too much to take on such a commitment. Both types are intelligent and quickly recover from adversity.

The wood Horse loves the great outdoors.

The fire Horse (1966)

This is the most dreaded sign in Chinese astrology: fire Horses are adventurous – even reckless – confrontational, rebellious, unpredictable and loathe both commitment and any form of discipline (unless they are dishing it out). Relationships are a minefield, and it's a rare person who can put up with the wild fire Horse nature. Fire Horses need to use their intelligence and to be adaptable if they are to achieve happiness.

The earth Horse (1978)

Indecisive earth Horses are sometimes too logical for their own good. After weighing up all of the arguments, they tend to become stuck in a morass of confusion, often needing the guidance of others. Their essential insecurity may be masked by a tendency to act bossily. Sadly, their families don't seem to help them much, and friends often take the place of relatives. Often pretty wild when young, earth Horses mature well.

Novelty-seeking metal Horses yearn for excitement.

The metal Horse (1930, 1990)

The novelty-seeking metal Horse is restless, self-centred and never boring. This may put a strain on relationships, but on the level of friendship the metal Horse is always welcome company. This type needs an adrenaline rush and constant excitement to stave off the dreaded boredom. Usually able to live the good life, this Horse loves to make a show and isn't afraid of controversy or arguments.

The water Horse is a good listener and an excellent communicator.

The water Horse (1942, 2002)

A difficult start in life often impels the water Horse to become a success in later life. Competitive by nature, this Horse is a great traveller, generally athletic and ready for adventure. As well as being a good listener, the water Horse is a communicator, although inconstancy can create problems in close relationships. As a friend, the water Horse is an entertaining companion.

The year of the Horse

The Horse likes friendly people who are honest and have flair.

The optimistic Horse year bodes well for enterprising people, as long as they can adapt to sudden changes and take advantage of new opportunities. Only plans that have already been set in motion are likely to succeed, however, because this period is concerned with building on that which has been established, as well as preserving the best features and accomplishments of previous years. It is therefore unwise to instigate any major changes or formulate long-term plans during the Horse year. The Horse favours people who have a sense of flair and honest, independent attitudes, the essential integrity of the Horse also ensuring that personal peccadilloes will be publicly, and embarrassingly, aired. The Horse year may improve general well-being, with the result that troubling health issues may be resolved.

The fortunes of the Horse

Unlike most other signs, equine types don't have it all their own way during their year, the year of the Horse. In fact, the going could become even tougher than normal. The challenges that you now face will become a rapid learning curve, however, the trials and tribulations that you'll experience standing you in good stead throughout the rest of the twelve-year cycle. Although this is a year of transition, it's not yet time to ditch the old: make plans, but don't implement them until you are safely in the year of the Sheep.

The Horse will feel safer and more comfortable during the **year of the Sheep**, a calming atmosphere of contentment soothing your worries away. The going will be easier in all areas of your life, and you'll feel that you can at last make some progress. The career picture will improve as, indeed, will your love life, as a result of some of your stallion-like wildness having ebbed away, along with the feeling that you have something to prove.

The **year of the Monkey** offers the Horse excitement and a multitude of options. Although you'll have to draw on your accumulated experience in order to act wisely, you can't fail to be a success. It's time to take a gamble or two, not all of which will pay off, but you'll have fun however they turn out. The only downside to the Monkey year is the remote possibility of a family loss.

The **year of the Rooster** brings discipline to the Horse, which you know is good for you, but will probably resent. Only sensible decisions will succeed this year, so there should be no monkeying about! You will have the chance to increase your prosperity through prudent planning, enhance your love life through commitment and add to your personal prestige through being sober and reliable.

There's no point in the Horse being selfish during the **year of the Dog**: caring for others is the theme of the year, and only unwise steeds put their own interests first. This is the year in which the poor Horse will not be a racer, instead having to be content with pulling a plough. Because the Dog year highlights emotions, even previously isolated Horses will now be forced to share their feelings.

The headstrong Horse had better rein itself in when the **year of the Pig** arrives – its usual love of risk-taking is not advisable now. There will be many variables this year, and not all of them will be to the Horse's

The Horse should take a gamble or two in the Monkey year.

There is a remote possibility of a family loss in the year of the Monkey.

advantage. Take life as quietly as you can because there are just too many potential accidents and unpleasant coincidences in store to race ahead regardless.

The **year of the Rat** is the worst of all for the noble Horse, who will be confused by the devious rodent's underhand scheming and made to feel vulnerable. Your best-laid plans will go awry and you'll have more than one battle on your hands. All in all, try to keep your head down during the Rat year and don't spend your resources – you'll be needing them soon.

The love life could be troublesome in the year of the Ox.

Blessed relief comes with the **year of the Ox** (but not the water Ox, which is likely to be a little more uncomfortable). Ox years favour those who work hard, and the Horse being no stranger to diligence, you'll feel that you are at last getting somewhere and that your efforts are not in vain. However, love is not well starred and new affairs are likely to be disappointing.

The Horse's personal prosperity should improve during the **year of the Tiger**, and if Horses sensibly speculate to accumulate they should do well. Doorways of opportunity will beckon, and the typical Horse won't think twice about bolting through them. It is advisable to think before you act, however, because some of these doorways lead to dead ends and the last thing you want is to be distracted from your true aims.

The **year of the Hare** should be a time of exceptional good fortune for the Horse (even though the Hare is counted as an 'enemy'). Widen your horizons in all areas of your life and you should meet with success. Indeed, every venture should be a triumph for the

The Horse's prosperity will improve in the Tiger year.

Horse, who may feel the urge to make more of a mark on the world. Some Horses will take the world stage by storm, either in the entertainment industry or in politics.

The Horse will find that there are plenty of opportunities for fun in the highly social Dragon year.

Like its predecessor, the **year of the Dragon** is one of opportunity for the Horse. It won't always be easy, but dutiful Horses should maximise their efforts, as well as keeping an eye open for unexpected chances. Hard work and unremitting effort aren't the full story, however, and your social life should be fun-filled during the Dragon year. The only potential fly in the ointment is the Horse's capacity for tactlessness, but if you keep that under control you should be laughing.

Temptation is in the air throughout the alluring **year of the Snake**. It would be an iron-willed Horse who could resist it, and few Horses will try to. You'll have a wicked glint in your eye, and where your eye goes your body will surely follow. This tendency could cause havoc within your family, however, so try to hold yourself back. Don't mistake dreams for reality and try to be practical.

The Sheep

THE SIGN OF ART

1931, 1943, 1955, 1967, 1979, 1991, 2003, 2015

LOVERS
the talented Sheep easily finds happiness with the Horse, the refined Hare and the sympathetic Pig.

FRIENDS
there is an affinity with Tigers, Dragons, Snakes, Monkeys, Roosters and other Sheep.

ENEMIES
the imaginative Sheep usually leaves the plodding Ox far behind. The Sheep is also driven to distraction by the frequently gloomy Dog. In Chinese almanacs it is stated, 'The Sheep and the Rat quickly separate'.

WESTERN ZODIAC EQUIVALENT
Cancer (the Crab).

RULING PLANET
the moon, known in Oriental terminology as the 'great Yin'.

LUCKY GEM
emerald.

SYMBOLISM
creativity, art, social status and career success.

The characteristics of the sheep personality

The studious sheep personality is often slightly reserved – even shy – as well as good-natured, patient and reliable. Although capable of taking on an enormous workload, Sheep must be careful that they don't make themselves ill with stress-related complaints. Sheep people are often to be found working in the arts or the media, as writers or in professions involving health care. They have creative, somewhat dreamy, minds and deeply sensitive natures. This sensitivity can make them so vulnerable that they will protect their innermost feelings with a display of apparent indifference. Don't be fooled, however: no one (not even the Pig) is softer and more delicate than the Sheep. Facing confrontations and critical people is the Sheep's idea of hell; easily embarrassed, and very shockable, Sheep shy away from the vulgar and the brash. The best side of their character is found in their caring, loving attitude. Their values are based on a spiritual, rather than material, plane and they are not envious or vindictive in any way. Sheep have a superb sense of style, natural grace and an attractive, yet unassuming, personality.

The wood Sheep (1955, 2015)

Although wood Sheep are often afflicted with unhelpful families, they may inherit money and property. The best word to describe wood Sheep is decent: fair play is of paramount importance to them, a trait that shines forth from them and is appreciated by all. Like most Sheep, they are creative, artistic and lovers of nature. They are generally lucky in relationships and will probably have several children.

Wood Sheep often have unhelpful families, yet usually inherit property.

The fire Sheep (1967)

Commitment is an appalling concept to fire Sheep, at least in early life. Often eccentric, these Sheep are drifters who are content to dream their way through life. As may be expected, although money flows towards them, it flows away again equally quickly. As they get older, however, many of their ideas begin to take form, and fire Sheep have the intelligence and patience to see them through to the end.

The earth Sheep (1979)

Hard-working earth Sheep can be described as the salt of the earth. They are straightforward, trustworthy and stable people, with a streak of sensitivity, whose efforts will bring them prosperity. The creative side to the Sheep is evident in their character, especially when they can share their tastes with like-minded people. Earth Sheep hate lying and may therefore be too honest for their own good within relationships.

The metal Sheep (1931, 1991)

Despite possessing strong emotions, stylish, elegant metal Sheep are a bit of a mystery to others because they will not readily reveal their inner selves. This is a self-preservation strategy because although metal Sheep like to appear to be cool sophisticates, they are actually very vulnerable and easily wounded. It is this emotional need that also makes this type very demanding of a lover's attention.

The water Sheep (1943, 2003)

Insecure water Sheep desperately need love and approval and will go to great lengths to get it. This type hates to upset anyone and will therefore meekly follow the flock. Water Sheep generally hate change of any kind and would prefer not to be too noticeable. As they get older, however, they tend to overcome this shyness and make a remarkable success of themselves. They are both loveable and excellent communicators, but far too modest.

The year of the Sheep

The kindly Sheep is an omen of peace, so crises – both domestic and international – will be resolved during this harmonious period. The Sheep is particularly responsive to the needs of the masses during this, the most compassionate

There is a likelihood of a medical breakthrough or two in the year of the compassionate Sheep.

of the Oriental years. Humane people will rise to positions of authority and will instigate much-needed reforms, while there is also a likelihood of medical breakthroughs and scientific advances which will both help the populace and advance the frontiers of human knowledge. A radical new fashion trend could be a major feature of a Sheep year because where one sheep leads the whole flock will unquestioningly follow. Emotional contentment is another happy influence during this year, making it a good one in which to marry or to renew a flagging relationship. The outlook is not good if you wish to end a romantic liaison, however, perhaps because the clannish Sheep disapproves of divorce.

The year of the Sheep is a good one in which to marry or rescue an ailing relationship.

The fortunes of the Sheep

When the Sheep is in its own year, past diligence will be rewarded. This is an excellent year in which you can be you, without enduring any carping or criticisms from others. Your self-questioning, anxious tendencies will be less evident and you will feel a renewed confidence, making you extremely attractive and popular with others. This is the time to make major, life-changing decisions, so be bold and make them!

There's too much to confuse the Sheep during the zany **year of the Monkey**. The best that can be said about this year is that you won't be bored and, in fact, will probably be greatly amused by the follies going on around you. Make sure that you aren't equally foolish, though. Look after your own interests, don't be too trusting, hang onto your resources and try not to take risks during this unpredictable time.

The **year of the Rooster** could devastate the Sheep's delicate ego. Because the Rooster is very demanding by nature, you may believe that all but the simplest tasks are

The year of the Rooster can be very trying to the Sheep's delicate ego.

The characteristics of the Monkey personality

The lively Monkey is rarely, if ever, boring company. Fast-thinking, witty and exciting personalities, Monkeys yearn for a life of constant variety filled with new and stimulating people with whom they can have adventures. Their active intelligence means that they are quick on the uptake and are often intuitive, allowing their minds to operate almost independently of their consciousness to arrive at an answer to a question swiftly. The quick mental processor that is their brain is also particularly impatient, Monkeys becoming extremely irritated by slower-witted people. Monkeys are noted for their wicked tongues, too, their sarcasm being one of their less appealing features. These nimble simians are also rather resentful of authority and tend not to cope well in large organisations. This is not to say that they are not hard workers, but it is probably better for them if they are self-employed and can set their own speedy pace. Their independent nature is not reflected in their emotional lives, however: Monkeys desperately want to give and receive love and need a partner who will provide a steadying influence.

Monkeys usually prefer an independent life and are often self-employed.

The wood Monkey (1944, 2004)

Like other Monkeys, wood types tend to be restless and to live unsettled lives when young. They have inventive minds and are not afraid of a challenge. As they mature, they become very canny, shrewd in business and innovative in their thinking. Marriages later in life tend to be more successful than earlier emotional relationships, and some wood Monkeys need firm guidance from their partners.

Fire Monkeys are very competitive and do not hesitate to push others out of the way to achieve their goals.

The fire Monkey (1956, 2016)

The unpredictable nature of the fire Monkey has a touch of glamour about it. Dazzling, domineering and passionate, this Monkey is destined for higher things. With no apparent effort, they defeat challenges and push others out of their way. Their clever Monkey brains are adept at making money, mainly because they have a terrible fear of poverty. In love, fire Monkeys tend to be fickle.

The earth Monkey (1968)

The clannish natures of earth Monkeys ensure that they show protectiveness and generosity to those that they love, although they can ignore the needs of relative strangers. This trait may also become evident within a long-lasting partnership, when earth Monkeys can appear uncaring. Very quick and clever, these Monkeys can be naughty or roguish, but if they can stick to one thing for long enough their success should be guaranteed.

The metal Monkey (1980)

This type of Monkey is extremely passionate and possessive, hard-working and ambitious. Their ambition is not always selfish in nature, however, and metal Monkeys are as likely to be involved in raising funds for charitable causes as in accumulating cash for themselves. Their passions may also be philosophical rather than physical, metal Monkeys being devoted to their strongly held beliefs.

The water Monkey (1932, 1992)

Water Monkeys are shrewd, self-willed, capable and attractive. Born negotiators, they are often found working in the role of agent or business representative. Original, bold and stylish, water Monkeys are quite capable of talking themselves into trouble, but also of talking themselves out of it! Their curiosity will impel them to travel the world. Water Monkeys often marry well and have good relationships with their families.

Water Monkeys are skilled negotiators and make good agents, salesmen and representatives.

The year of the Monkey

Flirtatious people will have a whale of a time in the year of the Monkey.

Your resolution at the beginning of the year of the Monkey should be to make no long-term plans at all because the unpredictable nature of this simian sign will ruin the best-laid schemes, often before they've even got off the ground. This doesn't mean that successes aren't possible, however, far from it: there's certainly a chance of making a quick buck, but there's an equal chance of losing your gains as swiftly as you made them. Although the Monkey is happiest in the heady world of romance, even this area will be subject to the erratic moods of our outrageously cheeky friend. The flirtatious will have a whale of a time, but for those who prefer a more staid and settled relationship, the outlook could be disappointing. During the year of the Monkey the world is ready for the new, the unusual and the downright eccentric. Ideas that would not have been given an airing in previous years will now be joyfully considered.

The fortunes of the Monkey

The Monkey in its own year is in its element, leaping from one thing to another, from subject to subject, person to person, and even lover to lover. At last you can cast off all thoughts of heavy responsibilities and have lots of fun! Any enterprise that you begin is destined for success, especially since your capacity for long-term planning, not to say cunning, is on top form.

Be slightly suspicious during the **year of the Rooster** and you won't go far wrong. Be ready for anything, don't take too much on trust, and don't make the mistake of assuming that if someone is friendly he or she is also honest, otherwise you'll have cause to regret your openness. This is also a year for weighing up the importance of those closest to you, so don't neglect your nearest and dearest.

Monkey people's finances will probably receive a few blows during the dour **year of the Dog**, their exuberance and love of fun also becoming somewhat muted by the cynical atmosphere. Relationships won't be well-starred either, with people whom you thought you could rely on through thick and thin being preoccupied with their own worries and tending to let you down in all sorts of ways. The Monkey is nothing if not resilient, however, and you will bounce back!

The Monkey must be prepared for hard work in the year of the Pig.

If you are a wise Monkey, you'll work very hard during the **year of the Pig**. Although the general keynotes of the year are peace, prosperity and purity, you'll feel rather left out of the equation and a less attractive side to your personality may emerge as you become resentful of other people's good fortune. Try to rise above such petty concerns: your time will come, so reserve your biggest plans for the forthcoming Rat year.

The Monkey's finances are set to bloom in the year of the Rat.

Lady Luck will smile upon the merry Monkey during the **year of the Rat**, when all of the good things that you've felt you've been missing out on will be coming your way. Your plans will prosper, your financial fortunes will bloom and as for your romantic life, well, it would be hard to resist the charms of the Monkey who is under the influence of such a compatible sign. The right sort of people will be attracted to you and will influence you in a very positive and progressive way.

Ever-curious Monkeys can improve their education in the intellectual atmosphere of the Dragon year.

Although the going won't be easy during the **year of the Ox**, Monkeys should make the most of the opportunities that come their way. You are unlikely to feel too optimistic, however, since your sense of fun will not be appreciated by the world in the course of this serious, dutiful year. In the meantime, seize the chance to learn a thing or two to while away the boredom. You never know: some of your new-found skills may come in useful during the forthcoming Tiger year.

It's another sunny forecast when the **year of the Tiger** dawns, when good luck should be an ever-present feature of your life. Too much of a good thing could make you lazy and complacent, however, but if you can avoid that pitfall the Tiger year should be plain sailing. Many Monkeys will find themselves in a position of influence, probably in some sort of advisory capacity.

The **year of the Hare** continues the Monkey's good fortune and could bring a measure of personal happiness, too. You are likely to feel more at ease with yourself and to realise that you have achieved something worthwhile. This doesn't mean that you should rest on your laurels, however, but that you should use your influence to further your cause throughout the Hare year. Call in a few favours in order to smooth your path through life.

The outlook for the **year of the Dragon** is excellent, especially if ever-curious Monkeys are prepared to put a little more effort into improving their education. Many Monkeys will take up a course of study or seek to expand their careers, possibly also travelling to broaden their knowledge. There will be some expensive times in the offing, however, so beware of squandering your resources.

Tread carefully during the **year of the Snake**! It will be all too easy for chattering Monkeys to make serious enemies who will not be inclined to forgive or forget their indiscretions. On the other hand, Monkeys aren't likely to care about this and will be able to handle any opposition. Take especial care in your love life and try not to become involved in an eternal-triangle scenario. Risk may be exciting, but it is also dangerous.

The **year of the Horse** won't be conducive to the expression of the Monkey's true nature. In fact, you'll find that it's best to keep a low profile and allow the year's turbulent and unpredictable events to pass you by. Respectability and the Monkey don't often go together, but it's advisable to brush up your image during the Horse year. Because your sympathies will be aroused by many worthy causes, keep your finances under particularly strict control.

The **year of the Sheep** should be a good year for Monkeys, during which they can sort out their lives. If you have got yourself into a pickle emotionally or financially, your active mind and creative approach to the problem will soon resolve it. If money has been a worry, learn from your past mistakes: be more careful with your cash in future and don't make a wanton display of your wealth.

A creative approach to cash problems will stand Monkeys in good stead in the Sheep year.

雞 The Rooster

THE SIGN OF CANDOUR

1933, 1945, 1957, 1969, 1981, 1993, 2005, 2017

LOVERS

the Rooster will find stability in relationships with the Snake, the Ox and the Dragon.

FRIENDS

the Rooster's sense of style wins appreciation from Tigers, Horses, Sheep, Monkeys and Pigs.

ENEMIES

the candid Rooster loathes the pretensions of the Hare and the indiscretions of the Rat. In Chinese tradition, it is said that two Roosters cannot share a house in harmony, and also that 'The Cock sheds tears at the sight of the Dog'.

WESTERN ZODIAC EQUIVALENT

Virgo (the Virgin).

RULING PLANET

Mercury, known in China as the 'little regulator' or the 'water star'.

LUCKY GEM

pink jasper.

SYMBOLISM

Because it is said that 'The Cock frightens demons, who fly at the sight of his red comb', the Rooster is thought to keep evil spirits and misfortune at bay.

The characteristics of the Rooster personality

Roosters love glamour and the social scene. To a Rooster, fun must involve flirtation.

People born under the sign of the flamboyant Rooster have extremely lively minds and can achieve a great deal through study and being generally well read. Cheerful, novelty-loving and broad-minded, Roosters are also outgoing, make friends easily and talk around the clock. In addition, they are glamorous and enjoy being in the thick of the social scene. On the minus side, Roosters can be conceited, opinionated and boastful, although they are not prone to bearing grudges or to long periods of sulking. They cannot bear dull-witted people, however, and expect their companions to have minds as lively as their own. To a Rooster, fun must involve flirtation, along with the chance to show off a little. Yet however eccentric and original Roosters may be, they are also very organised– perhaps a little too organised, Roosters being reputed to be difficult to live with. That having been said, there is no doubt that Rooster people are decent and honourable and that when they finally settle down they will be faithful and caring, although though their flirtatious tendency won't be curbed. Early family life may be difficult for Roosters, their families often being of little help to them. Roosters' true destiny lies far from their points of origin, frequently in the arts or armed forces (Roosters love uniforms).

Roosters love uniforms, and many join the armed forces.

The wood Rooster (1945, 2005)

Wood Roosters demand that things are done their way or not at all! Although exacting, these Roosters, like many others, are fair, decent and honest. They can, however, be annoying, especially when they talk endlessly about their pet subjects. Their passion extends beyond words, because wood Roosters are also ardent lovers.

The fire Rooster (1957, 2017)

There is no doubt that fire Roosters are leaders. Often found working in the media, running a successful business or charting a wholly independent course, fire Roosters are always going to be noticed. Intense, talented, persevering, excitable and self-motivated, they are destined for the top and may also inherit money or receive a windfall. Fire Roosters make friends easily, but are not so successful in the romantic stakes.

The earth Rooster (1969)

The Rooster brilliance becomes more stable, systematic and analytical when the element of earth is added to the mix. Earth Roosters are excellent organisers and financial managers. They can be very opinionated, however, a tendency which may alienate others. This type of Rooster desperately needs emotional security and may marry young in an attempt to find it.

The metal Rooster (1981)

Although fame is the destiny of a metal Rooster person, this does not necessarily translate into financial fortune. Metal Roosters have sharp tongues, are quite abrasive and can talk themselves out of the things that should rightfully be theirs. They may be idealistic and hard-working, but their intrinsic moodiness makes them unreliable and difficult to get along with.

The water Rooster (1933, 1993)

If a go-between is needed, look no further than an eloquent water Rooster: this Rooster is at home with any form of communication, be it writing or talking – lots! Superb organisers and persuaders, water Roosters can turn the most implacable of enemies into the fondest of friends, and vice versa. Real culture-vultures, wood Roosters are fond of art and music.

The year of the Rooster is good for those who wish to advance their careers.

The year of the Rooster

The year of the strutting Rooster should be an excellent period for people who want to advance their careers, gain a higher status in society or achieve prominence in any creative field. Accept all

challenges in the knowledge that you have all that you need in order to overcome them and triumph. Like the Monkey who rules the preceding year, the Rooster is fond of the new, which means that this year will give another chance to air the unusual, the unorthodox and the outrageous. A new interest will be apparent in these strange ideas, even if they were previously rejected. The Rooster loathes disorganisation, so where chaos once reigned, a different, sublime order will be established. This new set of rules will regulate most areas of life smoothly, although when it comes to relationships the opposite is likely to be the case. Some partnerships may be put under strain as a result of one partner starting to assert more independent attitudes.

The fortunes of the Rooster

You'll always know exactly where you are when the Rooster is in its own year. Your bank account may be stretched, but this will not be a worry because your earning potential will be considerably boosted. This is the time to plan your next moves, as well as the ones after that and, indeed, to calculate your way through life far into the future. While doing this, why not relax and treat yourself to a marvellous – and much-needed – holiday?

Treat yourself to a glorious and much-needed vacation in the Rooster year.

The **year of the Dog** is not an auspicious time for the Rooster's high-flying dreams of glory to be attained. It will be hard work all the way, and even you will have to admit that when harsh realities are inescapable the only way to cope is to knuckle down to the job in hand. You may have to scratch around for a living for a while, but succeed you eventually will. At least you will be needed – by nearly everybody – and usually at the most inconvenient moments.

Nothing worthwhile will be easy to achieve during the **year of the Pig**. If you are a typical Rooster, you will distrust the year's easy-going atmosphere, suspecting that something fishy is going on. And you will probably be right! Your emotional life is likely to be troublesome, with your tolerance being stretched to breaking point on occasion. At least challenges will be fewer during the Pig year, although the chances of reward will be, too.

Roosters who are fond of gambling will have a hard time during the **year of the Rat**, which is not a good one in which to take risks, even though you'll tend to think that your chances of

winning are high. Even if you do make some short-term gains, it is doubtful whether you will be able to keep them. Sensible planning, sound investments and a little self-denial are the only ways in which to achieve anything during this period.

Although when Roosters find themselves in the **year of the Ox**'s compatible sign favours will be rarely given, they will not be obstructed either. Ox years always encourage hard work and diligence, but rarely favour fools or the lazy. Because you are neither foolish nor idle you will do well, especially if you make sure that your head rules your heart and not the other way around.

The Rat year has too many risks for the Rooster's comfort.

Too many sudden changes will occur to make a Rooster feel comfortable during the **year of the Tiger**. Your wits may be keen enough to keep up with the hectic pace, but that doesn't mean that you won't be exhausted by the emotional turmoil. Although you may feel like retiring from the world for a while and becoming a recluse, this is the last thing that you should do: surrendering now would mean failure, and you couldn't bear that!

Although it's likely that the Rooster will hate the idle pretences of the **year of the Hare**, the generally calm atmosphere will soothe your spirits and help you to recover some of your composure. Stick to what you know, expect little in the way of prominence or glory and just get on with the job in hand. Any romantic inclinations will go unfulfilled this year, so keep your mind on practical matters.

The hectic pace of the Tiger year will emotionally exhaust the fraught Rooster.

There's a chance to show off during the **year of the Dragon**, when the flamboyant Rooster can get out into the world and make a stunning impact. The approval that many Roosters have long craved should now be apparent, so make the most of it. The Dragon year is also a great time in which to begin a new activity, start a business or tie the knot.

The flamboyant Rooster will win appreciation and applause in the Dragon year.

Because the Rooster is under the influence of a compatible sign during the **year of the Snake**, good fortune is forecast. Self-assertion being the key to success, strutting Roosters should be happily pushing themselves to the forefront, making as much fuss as they like and remembering to crow their own praises. You will stand out from the crowd and will be justly admired for your enterprise and courage. You'll inevitably make some enemies, of course, but you simply won't care!

Health issues are to the fore in the Horse year. The Rooster should ditch some bad habits.

The year of the Dog

Careful investment is the key to success in the year of the prudent Dog.

This is not a year for going out on a limb or taking a gamble of any kind. Caution should be the watchword because there is danger in the air. The loyal Dog warns that this is a year in which you should be watchful, safeguard the security of your home and possessions, jealously guard all that you have gained and beware of risking it all in the vague hope that you might gain more. Your finances should be invested safely in something solid and boring and not risked on some glamorous venture that may turn out to be nothing more than hot air. Prudent financial planning should see benefits accrue through an increase in property values, but you will probably still see the sense in hanging on a little longer to see if there is extra profit to be had. The Dog year is good news for relationships: marrying now will ensure a lifetime's devotion.

The fortunes of the Dog

The Dog its own year will meet with good fortune: at last the world will be ready to appreciate your finer qualities, hear your views and act on them. You will be determined to make the world a better place and many of your ideals will be accepted. A lot of praise will come your way, and although it isn't your nature to swallow flattery whole, you should at least allow yourself a few moments of self-congratulation.

The **year of the Pig** will be one of relaxation for the busy Dog. Although you rarely allow yourself to slacken off, the Pig year may force you to do just that as an antidote to stress, and even you will have to admit that you would prefer a less pressurised existence. Don't resent taking time off: use this opportunity to enhance the more cultural, poetic side of your personality.

The Dog should take it easy, relax and enjoy the stress-free year of the Pig.

The wise Dog will stay out of the limelight during the **year of the Rat**. The overt materialism of this year will appal your finer feelings and offend your sense of justice, which means that it's time to step back and allow the world to go its own grubby way for a while. The Rat race is not for you, and you'll be happiest when you are as far away from it as possible.

Although the **year of the Ox** is all about hard work and striving for a worthy cause, the year's prevailing sense of practicality has little time for the idealism of the Dog. You may be no stranger to effort, but your often revolutionary ideas will win no favour now. The best that you can do is to try to fit in and not to rock the boat, otherwise the powers-that-be will attempt to stifle you and may even punish your presumption.

In contrast to the year of the Ox, the **year of the Tiger** will welcome the Dog's revolutionary zeal. In many ways the Dog and the Tiger are in tune, and for once the Dog will be happy with the fast and furious pace of events. Your self-esteem will shoot skywards and any battles that need to be fought will bring you victory. Your usual scepticism is nowhere to be seen, however, so be careful about who you believe and don't be led astray by flattery and wishful thinking.

The Dog will find the pace of life exhilarating in the fast and furious Tiger year.

The beginning of the **year of the Hare** will be generally difficult for Dog personalities because there'll be too much chasing around after things that simply won't be caught! Force yourself to calm down, take a breather and try to adopt a more philosophical viewpoint. As the year progresses, you'll be likely to find yourself acting in an advisory capacity, as well as prospering in the romantic stakes.

The prospects of romance are good for the Dog in the year of the Hare.

Dog personalities will have to toe the line during the **year of the Dragon** – there's no point in seeking the limelight because the Dragon reserves centre-stage for himself alone. A prudent Dog will listen to advice this year; there'll be plenty of that, and it will be sensible, too. Make sure that you remember it, because when your chance eventually comes you'd do well to apply the lessons that you've learned in order to maximise your advantage.

The Dog will need to take care during the **year of the Snake**, when there are likely to be many upheavals and upsets. Nothing will be straightforward, with deceptions and half-truths being a recurring theme. It may go against the grain, but you will have to be assertive to avoid being ground down by arrogant individuals. Don't be tempted to depart from the straight and narrow.

The **year of the Horse** will be full of minor worries, keeping the overly anxious Dog on its toes. Determination and self-confidence are the keys to success, so do not waver or allow your doubts to overwhelm you. On a more positive note, your material fortunes will generally improve throughout this nerve-wracking year.

The Horse year is nerve-wracking for Dogs, yet material fortunes will improve.

Feelings of insecurity will plague the Dog during the **year of the Sheep**, even though the outlook is actually quite good. You'd be well advised to consider issues of self-esteem and to avoid resorting to pills and potions to ease your troubled mind. Although you should exceed your expectations in matters of creativity and romance, even these triumphs will cause you extra worry. Try to be quiet, stick to your own space and work on perfecting yourself.

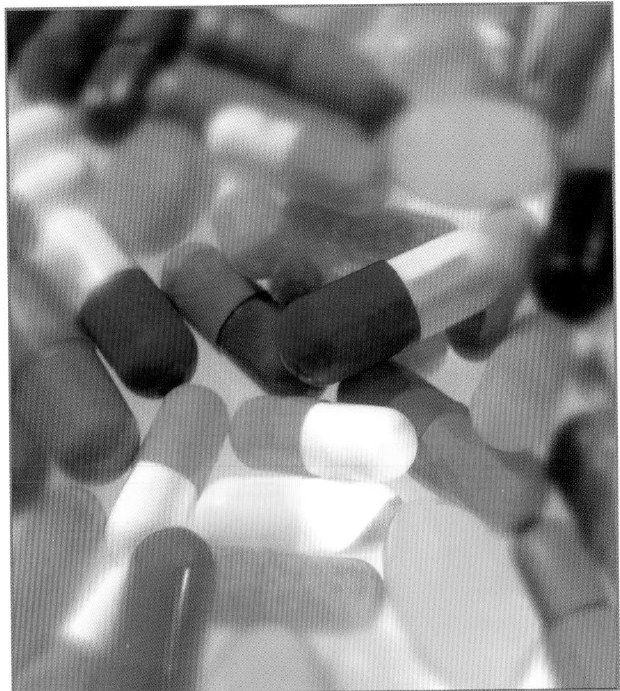

Dogs should not be tempted to resort to pills and potions to relieve stress in the Sheep year.

Those Dogs who can overcome their insecurity and take a small gamble will do well during the **year of the Monkey**, in which fortune favours the brave, a tip that Dog personalities would do well to remember. Good luck may strike an area of

your life that has been unsatisfactory, so take a risk, travel more, expand your horizons and, most importantly, don't be shy. Your courage will bring you great rewards.

Lessons in survival are the rule rather than the exception during the **year of the Rooster**, when the Dog's lofty idealism must take second place while harsh practicalities are addressed. This doesn't mean that you will lose your basic values, however, rather that you will temporarily have to bow to the prevailing necessities and get down to the nitty-gritty. The Rooster's cynicism may raise your hackles, but be patient: your year will soon come.

Dogs should take the opportunity to expand their personal horizons in the year of the Monkey.

猪

The Pig

THE SIGN OF HONESTY

1935, 1947, 1959, 1971, 1983, 1995, 2007, 2019

LOVERS

the refined tastes of the Hare, as well as the artistry of the Sheep, ensure a happy relationship with people of either sign.

FRIENDS

the Pig makes friends easily, particularly with Rats, Oxen, Tigers, Dragons, Horses, Roosters and Dogs.

ENEMIES

it is not considered advisable for Pigs to consort with other Pigs. The cunning Snake can also swallow a Pig whole, while ancient almanacs state that 'A Boar [Pig] and a Monkey will be quickly parted'.

WESTERN ZODIAC EQUIVALENT

Scorpio (the Scorpion).

RULING PLANET

traditionally Mars, the 'fire star', but now considered to be co-ruled by Pluto.

LUCKY GEM

topaz.

SYMBOLISM

wealth, family prosperity and general comfort. It is said that the Pig attracts happiness and good fortune.

The characteristics of the Pig personality

With their placid, gentle and retiring demeanour, it is almost impossible to dislike someone born in the year of the Pig. Don't be fooled, however: inside lies a will of iron and a swift assessment of other people's motives. Their honesty often being taken as naïvety, Pig people sometimes appear gullible and overly trusting, their awareness of their own sincerity often leading them to believe that others are equally sincere. Indeed, it is the rare Pig who has not suffered from advantage-takers at some stage in their lives. On a more positive note, Pig personalities are intelligent, dutiful and extremely capable. They prefer the status quo and will not rock the boat unless they are forced to do so. Pigs are intensely loyal to their families and close friends and can be very generous to those they love, denying themselves personal luxuries in order to do so (which may be why Pigs are frequently obsessive bargain-hunters). Pigs are also extremely sensual, a trait that some particularly amorous Pigs may take too far.

The wood Pig (1935, 1995)

Charitable wood Pigs are not destined for an easy time, yet their efforts to improve matters reveal advanced souls. Illness may have been a feature of their early lives or, equally likely, they may have difficulties with their own children. Although their home life may not be perfect, this is the area to which they devote most of their time and energy. Wood Pigs are at their best when working for other people's causes.

The fire Pig (1947, 2007)

Optimistic fire Pigs are lucky, having a talent for making a silk purse out of a sow's ear and turning apparently hopeless situations to their advantage. Happy to combine their work and home lives, fire Pigs often make great entertainers because their independent attitude gives them an unusual slant on life. These Pigs are very sensual, so a scandal or two surrounding them will not be unusual.

Fire Pigs are very happy to combine their work and home lives.

The earth Pig (1959, 2019)

Putting other people's interests before their own is the hallmark of self-sacrificing earth Pig. These Pigs are very clannish and consistently put their family's well-being before their own. This can be a bad thing, however, both from the point of view of lost opportunities and because they can be unpleasant to those outside their immediate circle.

The metal Pig (1971)

Well-organised metal Pigs can often be bullies. Overbearing, demanding and somewhat insensitive, they will not accept opposition or the thwarting of their desires. At least these Pig gets things done! It may be their way or not at all, but there's no denying that their powerful determination is a force to be reckoned with. Particularly lucky when dealing with land or property, this Pig will go far. A later marriage will probably be more successful than an early one.

Metal Pigs can be overbearing, demanding and something of a bully.

The water Pig (1983)

Comfort, wealth and contentment is the destiny of water Pigs. Even if they were born in poverty, their ambition and persistence will enable them to accumulate resources. Some water Pigs are content with their material well-being, while others use their wealth to help others and prefer to focus on their quality of life rather than the number of possessions that they own. Water Pigs are good with children, very affectionate and basically cheerful.

Water Pigs are affectionate, cheerful, and very good with children.

The year of the Pig

Home improvement is one of the welcome developments in store for the Pig in his own year.

The last in the sequence of animal signs, the Pig year is the time to tie up loose ends, to assimilate what you have learned and to count your blessings before moving into the action-packed era of the Rat. Nostalgia is the keynote for this year, and many will find themselves looking back to happy days. Those who have squandered opportunities and messed up relationships will find their memories less comfortable companions, however. Because it marks the end of a cycle, there could be an air of celebration about the Pig year, with money perhaps being spent on home improvements or even a new house. Relationships and family issues are also well starred. In addition, for many people the year of the Pig will be a time of self-indulgence: indeed, some will make pigs of themselves and will leave no stone unturned in the pursuit of pleasure. Although Pig years are not noted for political upheavals, a revolution in the way in which people enjoy their leisure will not be out of the question.

There is the possibility that the Pig year heralds the start of a family.

The fortunes of the Pig

A sense of balance and perspective are a boon for the Pig in its own year, when you'll feel confident and ready for anything, while the universe will be throwing a lot of luck your way. Many Pig personalities will enter long-term emotional commitments, possibly starting a family or moving to a dream home, although some Pigs will receive the flattering attentions of a secret lover. Business affairs should flourish, too, with the promise of additional income.

The Pig's feeling of optimism should continue into the **year of the Rat**, although the sensible Pig should not become complacent because everything is going so well. Because the Rat year favours the enterprising, don't be distracted by the many pleasures that life offers and, in particular, keep your goal in your sights. You may not achieve it immediately, but your chances of eventual success are spectacular.

Although the **year of the Ox** will be one of diligence and hard work, the outlook continues to be good for the Pig. As long as you can maintain your pace, you will find others who share your aims and ambitions this year. The pleasure-loving side of your persona won't win any admiration, however, so beware of alienating your new allies by indulging yourself too much.

Pig personalities may not enjoy the revolutionary zeal of the **year of the Tiger**, preferring instead to stand back, await developments and amble gently on while attending to your own affairs. Having said that, nothing will stand in your way this year: the Tiger will be concerned with more important things than the doings of the Pig. In fact, you may even find that others envy your laid-back lifestyle during this turbulent time.

The **year of the Hare** should be excellent for the Pig's personal finances. Although you may not know where the money is coming from, you'll certainly know where it's going: on your increasingly opulent lifestyle! If you are challenged in any way, you will win by force of personality alone, which means that engaging in confrontations and standing up for yourself will stand you in good stead.

The year of the Hare is good for the Pig's finances allowing an opulent lifestyle.

Continuing the theme of the previous year, the **year of the Dragon** should benefit the Pig's coffers. You may, however, develop some nagging doubts and become a shade more conscientious in your dealings with others. You'll probably be troubled by the feeling that something unsavoury is going on and, worse still, that you may be an unwitting part of it. The changes are being rung this year, and you'll be left with the impression that the good times won't last forever.

The **year of the Snake** is not likely to be comfortable for the gentle Pig – snakes eat pigs, so be careful! Emotional vulnerability is the keynote this year, which means that it is not the time to wear your heart on your sleeve. Any new people that enter your life are likely to be false and demanding, so practice saying 'No!' loudly and clearly. Certain mysterious happenings will make you feel even more anxious throughout the slippery Snake period.

The sensitive Pig can settle down during the **year of the Horse**, which brings an atmosphere of calm. Having endured a number of traumas, you'll now be ready to catch your breath and recover a little. You may be wondering where to go from here, in which case the Horse year will probably involve a lot of self-questioning and the occasional moan, but by the end of it there'll be a hint of romance and you'll be feeling emotionally fulfilled.

The year of the Snake is not one for the sensitive Pig to wear his heart on his sleeve.

A love affair is likely to be established or renewed in the year of the Sheep.

A distinct lack of competition will be evident during the **year of the Sheep**, which will please Pig personalities and add to their happiness considerably. Your financial fortunes are likely to be steady, controllable and notable for the contentment that they bring. Contentment will be found in emotional ways, too, with a love affair being established or renewed. Bask in this period of mental peace and build up your strength for the intrigues to come.

The **year of the Monkey** will keep you on your toes, but will also be a period during which you'll be happy to wheel and deal and to sample some politics and intrigue. Although you may not even have known that you had it in you, it will seem as though you've been a player all of your life. High stakes also involve high risks, of course, but as long as you're prepared you should do well. Be your own person and make your own decisions.

Pigs will wheel and deal for high stakes in the intriguing year of the Monkey.

Although the Pig's spending habits will undergo a radical rethink during the **year of the Rooster**, you should essentially approve of the changes. In your heart of hearts you know that a lesson in economy has been long overdue, so you won't resent the strictures that this year imposes on you. A quieter, more controlled, life could be just what you need to enable you to indulge some of your cultural tastes.

The **year of the Dog** will be full of crusades, which the Pig won't be altogether comfortable with, the repetition of strident slogans tending to get on your nerves. If you want a happy life when everyone around you seems bent on achieving their lofty goals, keep your head down, attend to your own concerns and try to keep the world at bay.

Index

Bibliography

Dee, Jonathan, *Feng shui*, Caxton, 1999.

Dee, Jonathan, *Feng shui for the garden*, Caxton, 2000.

Dee, Jonathan, *Feng shui from scratch*, D&S Books, 2001.

Dee, Jonathan, *Chinese face reading*, D&S Books, 2001.

Barry Fantoni, *Chinese horoscopes*, Sphere, 1985.

Fenton, Sasha, *Chinese divinations*, Zambezi, 2001.

Hean-Tatt, Ong, *Chinese animal symbolisms*, Pelanduk, 1993.

Huon de Kermadec, Jean-Michel, *The way to Chinese astrology*, Unwin, 1986.

Rigby, Paul, and Bean, Harvey, *Chinese astrologics*, Yee Tin Tong.

Sachs, Robert, *Nine star Ki*, Element, 1999.

Selene, Predicting your future, *Salamander*, 1989.

Walters, Derek, *Chinese astrology*, Aquarian, 1987.

Walters, Derek, *The Chinese astrology workbook*, Aquarian, 1988.

White, Suzanne, *Chinese astrology*, Pan, 1993.

Credits & Acknowledgements

Picture top left p7 © D&S Books.

All other photographs © Stockbyte

All illustrations by Pauline Cherrett